# Why is Britain becoming harder to govern?

Based on the BBC1 series *Politics Now*

Anthony King
David Coates
Norman St John-Stevas
John P. Mackintosh
Samuel Brittan

**Edited by Anthony Ki**

GW00391460

BRITISH BROADCASTING CORPORATION

Published to accompany three television programmes first shown on BBC1 at 11.05 p.m. on the 15, 22 and 29 February, 1976.

The three programmes form a unit 'Why is Britain becoming harder to govern?' in the series *Politics Now*.

*Politics Now* was produced by Bernard Adams and Judy Harris.

Published to accompany a series of programmes prepared in consultation with the BBC Further Education Advisory Council.

Published by the British Broadcasting Corporation, 35 Marylebone High Street, London W1M 4AA

This book is set in 10pt Linotype Baskerville Roman

Printed in England by Love & Malcomson Ltd, Redhill, Surrey. ISBN 0 563 10999 8

# Contents

# Foreword

The change that has come over Britain in the past ten years or so is really rather frightening. During the 1960s people in Britain – or at least the politically attentive among them – got used to the idea that the British economy was not growing as fast as the German, French or Japanese, and was unlikely to grow as fast in the future. It seemed that Britain was set for a fairly long period of relative economic decline. This was mildly disturbing. Few of us like to see our neighbours growing richer faster than we are, and the politicians, in particular, were conscious that the balances between public and private expenditure and between consumption and investment are more easily struck in a rapidly than in a slowly expanding economy.

But for most people it was not more than mildly disturbing. After all, the country's economy, although growing slowly, was growing nevertheless. Britain's relative poverty was an abstraction, something one read about in the newspapers. The reality was of an unprecedented level, in absolute terms, of prosperity. As one factory worker put it to his MP, 'If this is an economic crisis, I like it.' Equally important, even those who were conscious of Britain's relative decline, and worried about it, could console themselves with the thought that, although the management of the country's economy might leave something to be desired, Britain's affairs in other respects were managed rather well. In a world of mounting chaos and barbarism, Britain at least remained orderly and civilised. British prime ministers were not assassinated; gunmen did not shoot at passers-by from rooftops. And Britain's public services remained among the best in Europe, if not in the world. They were certainly far better than America's. To travel again on London's underground after a few weeks of riding on the New York subway – the noise deafening, the carriages daubed with paint, too many of the passengers looking discouraged, even afraid – was to be reminded that Gross National Product is not everything.

During the 1960s almost everyone took Britain's political institutions for granted. They needed to be reformed, of course. The civil service was thought to be too amateur; it was generally agreed that Parliament needed to be more responsive to the electorate and more capable of acting as a check on the executive. But no one advocated scrapping the constitution entirely, and most of us assumed, without really thinking about it, that our political system would remain essentially unchanged. Whatever else happened, the press would remain free, Parliament would go on sitting, the political parties would continue to contest elections. Britain would remain in the future what she had been in the past – a tolerant, liberal democracy.

Suddenly, in the mid-1970s, we are not so sure. We had got used to the crisis in our economy. Now we begin to wonder whether we are not also confronted with a crisis in our polity. Laws enacted by Parliament are not obeyed by the people. Elected Governments find that they have to share their power with unelected bodies like the Trades Union Congress and the Confederation of British Industry. Governments come and go with increasing frequency. Events are seemingly beyond their control. And the signs multiply of popular restlessness. Turnout at general elections has declined sharply since the early 1950s. So has support for both of the two major political parties. Men and women who have grievances, whether they be trade unionists or nursing sisters or dairy farmers, are far readier than they were a generation ago to take their grievances into the streets. Politically as well as economically, we in Britain can feel the ground shifting, ever so slightly, under our feet.

Talk of the end of liberal democracy in Britain is, of course, premature. Democratic norms are still almost uni-

6

versally accepted in Britain. Neither the extreme left nor the extreme right has anything remotely approaching either the mass following or the physical force that would be required to establish a dictatorship. Indeed serious talk of the end of British democracy is largely confined to American news magazines and television commentators. But the fact that the talk takes place at all is in itself remarkable. Britain is undoubtedly a much harder country to govern than it used to be – and is, if anything, becoming more so.

The question is : Why? Why is Britain becoming harder to govern? Is it simply the fault of the big trade unions, as so many people seem to think? Is it the fault of successive Conservative and Labour Governments? Or are there larger economic and political – and possibly even moral – forces at work? We decided, in connection with a series of BBC Television programmes, *Politics Now*, to be transmitted in early 1976, to put these questions to a number of politicians and political commentators. We knew that their answers would be tentative. We knew that they would be likely to disagree. We also knew that the answers they gave would be bound to be incomplete – and would ignore or neglect factors that other viewers or readers would deem to be important. But the questions seemed to us important to ask, and certainly no one we approached was disposed to disagree.

The answers that we got are set out in the five essays that make up this book. The five contributors worked largely independently of one another. They represent widely different parts of the political spectrum. In the following pages, each has set out his own answers in his own way.

# The problem of overload

Anthony King

Why has Britain become so much harder to govern over the past twenty years or so? It was once thought that Governments would be extremely difficult to remove from office, given their ability to manage the economy. Now we are inclined to assume the opposite: that the tenure of Governments is precarious and that for the foreseeable future it will be a lucky Government that survives for more than a term. It was once thought that Britain was an unusually easy country to govern, its politicians wise, its parties responsible, its administration efficient, its people docile. Now we wonder whether Britain is not perhaps an unusually difficult country to govern, its problems intractable, its people bloody-minded. What has happened? What has gone wrong?

This chapter suggests answers to these questions – or at least suggests places where answers might reasonably be looked for. It concerns itself with politics rather than economics, though obviously economics is important. Not all of the answers it offers are breathtakingly original. Given the amount of ink that has been spilt on this subject, it would be amazing if they were. But some of the answers will perhaps be new to some readers, and an effort has been made to formulate some of the old answers in new ways.

## The business of government more difficult

Let us begin by reminding ourselves of some of the indications that the business of government in Britain has become more difficult. The number of such indications is vast. A sampling of them can be listed, in no particular order.

In the 1960s the conventional wisdom had it that the country's local government system was badly in need of reform. There were too many local government units, they were of the wrong size, their functions were wrongly distributed among them, they were based on an out-of-date distinction between town and country. All sorts of benefits would accrue if the system were 'streamlined'. The system has now been streamlined, but somehow things are not working out quite as expected. The benefits from the new system are scarcely discernible; the costs have proved enormous. Quite apart from the costs of the changeover as such, the new system is proving much more expensive administratively than the old. Almost everyone who worked in the old system has had to be found a new job. Since virtually the same number of jobs is organised in fewer hierarchies, the number of jobs within each hierarchical structure is larger and the men at the top of each structure have to be paid more. It has proved a game of musical chairs. With the music stopped, only the ratepayers are left standing.

In the case of local government reform, successive Governments set out to achieve certain ends – 'efficiency' and 'democracy' – but failed to achieve them. In the case of the running of the National Health Service, an already existing relationship between politicians and doctors, has, as Mrs Barbara Castle's recent experience has shown, begun to disintegrate. The 'settlement of 1948' is no longer mutually acceptable. On the one hand, the Labour Government seeks to abolish pay beds in NHS hospitals and generally to diminish the role of private medical practice. On the other, the medical profession seeks to defend its position, both financially and administratively, at a time when the rate of increase in the NHS's resources has decreased sharply. In between, the ancillary workers have realised the strength of their bargaining position. For something like a quarter-century, between 1948 and 1973, the NHS was not 'a problem' so far as government was concerned. Now it is.

The same is true, though for different reasons, of higher

education. It takes an effort of will in 1976 to recall the atmosphere in which the Macmillan Government welcomed the Robbins proposals in 1962. It was then thought that there would be more than enough qualified students to fill the greatly expanded number of university places, that a rapid expansion of higher education would be egalitarian in its social effects and that it would benefit the economy. The only serious criticism of Robbins at the time – the claim that 'more' must inevitably mean 'worse' – was, as subsequent events have shown, misguided. Yet so were many of the claims made on Robbins' behalf. Students have ceased to come forward in the requisite numbers; Britain is not notably more egalitarian or notably richer. Indeed in 1976, on top of doubts about how higher education is to be financed, there are serious doubts about what its purposes are.

Our experience of incomes policy offers a different sort of example. In this case, everyone is clear what the purposes of such a policy would be, but no one knows how to go about producing a successful policy that will last. As successive Governments have discovered, all incomes policies, whether labelled 'voluntary' or 'compulsory', are in fact voluntary. As successive Governments have also discovered, everybody's interest is nobody's interest. It is wholly rational for any single group of workers to use its bargaining power to increase the level of its money wages even though the cumulative effect of all groups of workers using their power in this way may be to reduce the level of real wages of every one of them. In retrospect, the remarkable thing is not that incomes policy has failed to work in the 1960s and 1970s but that it worked at all in 1948–49.

The failure of incomes policy is obviously related to the failure of economic policy generally. It labours the obvious to point out that, whatever their aims – a high rate of growth, stable prices, a surplus on the balance of payments, a reduction in industrial unrest – post-war Governments have failed to achieve them, at least for any sustained period.

The only exception has been the maintenance of full employment but, in 1976, even that is seriously at risk. We have come a long way from the confident Keynesianism of the 1944 White Paper.

One further indication that the business of government has become more difficult is worth remarking on. It is the increasing difficulty that both major political parties seem to have in carrying out their election manifestos. The fit between what the Labour party said it would do in 1945 and what the Labour Government actually achieved between 1945 and 1951 is astonishingly close. Most of *Let us Face the Future*, Labour's manifesto in 1945, reads like a prospective history of the immediate post-war period. Since about 1959, however, the fit has become less close. Not only do parties in office increasingly fail to do the things they said they were going to do : they increasingly do things that they pledged themselves specifically not to do. The Heath Government became famous for its 'U-turns'. The present Wilson Government last year executed its own U-turn on incomes policy. Since there is no reason to believe that the political parties are any less serious now than they were after the war about what they say in their manifestos, there is every reason to suppose that somehow, in some way, the business of government has become harder to carry on in the intervening period.

Examples like the above could be multiplied indefinitely. One thinks of the growth of crime despite the best efforts of government, of the failure of economic planning, of the intractability of the Northern Irish problem, of the misguidedness, as it has turned out, of much recent energy policy – and so on, and on. Americans used to write of 'Big Government' as though the state, in becoming all-embracing, would become all-powerful. Today our image of government is more that of the sorcerer's apprentice. The waters rise. The apprentice rushes about with his bucket. The waters rise even faster. And none of us knows when, or whether, the magician will come home.

11

The argument of this chapter is that a large part of the explanation for this state of affairs can be stated in two propositions. Each of them is reasonably familiar in itself, though the first, as it happens, is more familiar than the second. What is not generally appreciated is what happens when both propositions turn out to be true at the same time.

The first, more familiar proposition is that the range of matters for which British Governments hold themselves responsible – and for which they believe that the electorate may hold them responsible – has increased greatly over the past ten or twenty years, as well as over the past fifty, and is still increasing at a rapid rate.[1] So rapid is the rate indeed that most of us, although aware of it, have become insensitive to it, just as citizens of certain countries have become inured to very high rates of price inflation. Take a simple example. When the calling of the October 1974 general election led to the cancellation of the annual Conservative and Labour party conferences, which were due to take place in Blackpool, the hoteliers and restaurateurs of that city petitioned the Department of Trade for compensation on the ground of the losses that they would incur. They were probably just trying it on; they cannot have been wholly serious. But it is highly significant that the idea occurred to them at all – even as a try-on. It would not have occurred to anyone in 1874 or 1924. It would probably not have occurred to anyone even in 1964. The hungry sheep look up and reckon that they have at least a reasonable chance of being fed. In so short a time has government come to be regarded, in Britain at least, as a sort of unlimited-liability insurance company, in the business of insuring all persons at all times against every conceivable risk.

It is instructive in this connection to re-read Herbert Morrison's *Socialisation and Transport*, published more than forty years ago.[2] The book represents the fruits of Morrison's thinking about the public corporation, based on his experience of creating the London Passenger Transport Board. It is a long book and in places quite a detailed one. Morrison had already had a good deal of political experience and was by instinct a political animal. Yet in this book Morrison completely fails to grasp the purely political – as distinct from the economic – consequences of greatly enlarging the public sector; or, rather, he grasps them but fails to realise that they cannot be avoided. In his discussion of the management of nationalised industries, he assumes 'that the management of these industries can broadly be relied upon to get on with its work, and having done one good deed the Minister can let the people put in charge carry on with the work done, while he immediately sets about the other good deeds of socialisation which await his attention.' Later on he explains why the 1929–31 Labour Government was reluctant to guarantee the LPTB's finances :

> The Government did not wish to do this for it might well have encouraged a spirit of slackness, or even recklessness, on the part of the Board in matters of management, on the part of the travelling public in demanding lower fares and uneconomic facilities, and on the part of the work people in asking for big concessions as to conditions of labour; all might be tempted to say 'Well, after all, the Treasury is behind us.'

Quite so. But there is more to it than that. It is not merely that a nationalised industry board may be slack or its customers want lower prices and its workers higher wages. More important is the fact that, in circumstances of intense electoral competition, when Governments hold themselves responsible (and are held responsible) for the management of the economy as a whole, they cannot not intervene in the affairs of nationalised industries. On the one hand, the affairs of the nationalised industries impinge directly on the lives of voters; and for what happens in these industries voters hold the Government of the day responsible, not the chairmen of the various boards. On the other hand, even if

13

Governments were not held responsible for the nationalised industries, they would be held responsible for managing the economy as a whole and, on political grounds alone, no Government could afford to deny itself one of its main means of controlling – or at least trying to control – the whole economy. The enlargement of the public sector has led to increased burdens being placed on government; the increased burdens placed on government have contributed to the enlarging of the public sector. In an era of incomes policy, investment policy, prices policy and regional policy, no Government, even if it wanted to, could in practice permit the management of the nationalised industries 'to get on with its work'. Morrison's mistake, his failure of political imagination, was not to realise that, when government becomes big, politics becomes big too.

This line of thought might once have been taken as anti-socialist – as an argument against taking industries into public ownership. Perhaps it is. But that is beside the point, which is that there is now hardly anything in which Governments can avoid taking an interest. The distinction between 'private' and 'public' has, as is well known, become hopelessly blurred. The border between the private and public domains resembles the border between New York and Connecticut far more than that between France and Germany (much less than between China and Russia). To be held responsible for everything is to feel compelled to intervene in everything. A Conservative Government rescues Upper Clyde Shipbuilders and nationalises part of Rolls-Royce; a Labour Government nationalises British Leyland and even picks up the pieces after the collapse of Court Line, a privately owned airline and holiday company that was not particularly important to the national economy. Public is still public; private in 1976 is also public.

A recent case whose significance has not been fully appreciated is that of the so-called sugar shortage in 1974. We have grown accustomed to looking to government to provide us with roads and water; we are growing accustomed to look to it to provide us with electricity and railway trains; we now, it seems, expect it to provide us with, of all things, sugar. The growing of sugar is in private hands; the refining of it is largely in private hands; the distributing and selling of it is wholly in private hands. Yet, when there is not enough of it in the shops, we look not to the growers, refiners or distributors to solve our problem but to Mr Fred Peart, i.e. to government. During the Irish potato famine, thousands of United Kingdom citizens could not count on government to provide them with life; today we expect government to provide us with sugar for our tea. The sugar shortage is a good case, and we will come back to it later.

Once upon a time, then, man looked to God to order the world. Then he looked to the market. Now he looks to government. The differences are important. God was irremoveable, immutable. The market could be removed or mutated but only, it was thought, at a very high price. Government, by contrast, is removeable, mutable – and corporeal. One blames not 'Him' or 'it' but 'them'. The Mass has given way to the general election, which is (to coin a phrase) a whole new ball game. How difficult a time Governments are having in trying to play God we shall see in the next section.

### The problem of intractability

Our first proposition was that Governments today are held responsible for far more than they ever were before. This in itself might not matter much if they were able to carry out their new responsibilities. It does not matter how many debts a man has if he has enough money in the bank or a good enough line of credit. But our second proposition is that, just as the range of responsibilities of Governments has increased, so, to a large extent independently, their capacity to exercise their responsibilities has declined. The reach of British government exceeds its grasp; and its grasp, according to our second proposition, is being enfeebled just at the moment when its reach is being extended.

It is easy to prove that this second proposition is true; it is more difficult to explain why it is true. The proofs lie all around us (some were mentioned earlier) : the failure to achieve a higher rate of economic growth, the failure to bring inflation under control, the failure to put right the balance of payments, the failure to build enough houses, the failure to reduce the level of violent crime, the failure to reform the trade unions, the failure to make a commercial success of Concorde. Almost the only unqualified success of British legislation in the past twenty years has been the Clean Air Act of 1956. Britain's buildings are indubitably cleaner.

Our first instinct, confronted with a record of failure, is to blame somebody – or, if we are political scientists, to blame institutions. And undoubtedly some of these failures can be laid at individuals' doors. The fault lies in our leaders and not in our stars that we failed to join the European Economic Community in the 1950s and therefore, perhaps, failed to join in Europe's economic growth. The fault lies with Mr Julian Amery and successive Ministers of Aviation, Technology, Trade and Industry, and Industry that Concorde was first conceived and then not aborted. The fault lies with Mr Harold Wilson that the pound was not devalued before 1967 when – who knows? – an earlier devaluation might have made a higher growth rate possible. The fault lies with all of our politicians that they have not, for example, established in Britain an Ecole Nationale d'Administration.

But clearly it will not do simply to blame our leaders or our institutions. Our leaders change, but Wilson's solutions, although different, turn out to be no better than Macmillan's, and Heath's solutions, although even more different, turn out to be no better than Wilson's. Our institutions change too, albeit slowly. A Department of Economic Affairs is created, then abolished. A Civil Service Staff College is set up. The Central Policy Review Staff is created. So are 'super-ministries'. But the problems remain, and grow worse. The suspicion grows that the difficulty lies not in the problem-solvers but in the nature of the problems. This suspicion is reinforced by the observation that, increasingly, Britain's problems are not peculiar to Britain. No free government has succeeded in winning the battle against inflation or the battle against crime. All governments are disoriented by the consequences of the sudden rise in Arab oil prices. The posture of modern statesmen is not, *pace* Giscard-d'Estaing, that of confident assertion but of mild bewilderment. We should ask why they are bewildered.

Let us consider four reasons why men and women might fail to achieve what they set out to achieve – four possible reasons for failure, all of them beyond the control of the individual would-be achiever.

1. One reason a man might fail is because what he set out to achieve was physically impossible to achieve, given current technology. Examples can be found, though with some difficulty, even in the 1970s. Rolls-Royce collapsed because the RB–211 aeroengine proved colossally expensive to develop – and was anyway clearly never going to function quite as intended because the engine's carbon-fibre propellor blades, despite their enormous pretensile strength, tended to break up on impact, even with objects as light as raindrops. There was nothing, in the short term, that Rolls-Royce's technicians could do about it. The company, given its fixed-price contract with Lockheed and promised delivery dates, went broke.

But such examples, although they can be found, are not common. Companies and governments do not normally set out to achieve the impossible or even what they have reasons for supposing may be impossible. More to the point, men have always been constrained by the physically impossible, more so in the past than now. The Carthaginians could not bomb Rome; the Duke of Wellington could not be interviewed on 'The World at One'. If failure seems to be assuming, as it does, new forms, the explanation cannot lie in old constraints, or at least not in them alone.

2. Another reason why a man or government might fail is simply because he or it lacked the necessary resources, or had to contend with too many claims on them. One reason why there are not enough houses in Britain (or in most other countries) is simply that available resources have been diverted elsewhere : construction workers to the building of motorways, bricks and cement to the building of office blocks and new universities. The problem of scarce resources is likely to be serious in most Western countries for the foreseeable future. In almost all non-Western countries it always has been. Given our low rate of economic growth, conflicts over resource allocation can be expected to be especially acute in Britain.

But, again, there is nothing new about the problem of scarcity, and it does not seem to offer an adequate, even plausible, explanation for the failure of local government reform, for the failure of incomes policy, for the failure of economic policy generally. It certainly cannot explain the almost universal feeling that the country has become harder to govern. Resources, after all, were far scarcer forty years ago when Britain seemed almost the only country that was relatively easy to govern. We must look further.

3. Another reason why someone might fail to achieve something is because he was dependent on someone else for the achieving of it and that other person failed, for some reason, to do whatever was required. A man who lives in the country but cannot drive a car may be dependent on his wife's ability and willingness to drive if he is to get to work on time. Most of us are dependent on the plumber to clear a blocked drain. We are all dependent on the compositors of Love & Malcomson (among others) for the printing of this book.

And here we come to the heart of the matter.[3] If Britain has become harder to govern, it is almost certainly partly because the number of dependency relationships in which government is involved has increased substantially, and because the incidence of acts of non-compliance by the other participants in these relationships has also increased substantially. Most of us are dependent not only on the plumber but also on the electrician, the carpenter, the heating engineer, our garage mechanic and the man who delivers the Sunday papers. If any one of them failed to turn up when we needed him, we could be in trouble. These two points are related empirically, very closely; but they are separate logically and we will deal with them separately.

First, the sheer number of dependency relationships – and the degree of dependence inherent in them. Though it is by now a cliché that our world has become increasingly interdependent, no one has attempted to estimate the number of relationships of dependence that exist. It must be enormous, running into thousands of thousands. The number has increased with the division of labour, the increases in standards of living, the increases in the scale and complexity of international trade. Governments are involved in a large proportion of these relationships. Sometimes they are directly involved, as purveyors of electricity supplies, medical services and (ideally) a stable currency. Sometimes they are indirectly involved, as when they are forced to respond to, without being able to control, the consequences of (say) foreign-exchange transactions between foreign nationals. The precise nature of the relationships varies. Britain is dependent on foreign suppliers for her imports of petroleum products and resinated wine; the petroleum products are more important than the wine. British government is dependent on the services of teachers in schools and teachers in universities; the school teachers' bargaining position is, as it happens, considerably more powerful than the dons'.

But for our purposes the details do not matter. The big picture does; so do its consequences. Some idea of the scale of change within living memory can be grasped if we compare – as seems reasonable to do – the miners' strike of February–March 1974 with the miners' strike of 1926. It is a little odd that the comparison was hardly made during the recent strike two years ago.

The 1974 strike lasted for rather less than a month, though it had been preceded by an overtime ban lasting several weeks. Its effects were felt immediately. The country's industry was put on a three-day week; there was a sharp fall in industrial production. Had the strike gone on much longer, power cuts would have been necessary despite the three-day week; the country's balance-of-trade deficit would have worsened greatly. Politically, the effects of the strike were even more spectacular. It destroyed an essential element in the Heath Government's economic policy, its Stage III incomes policy. It led directly (though perhaps not inevitably) to the holding of a general election and to the Heath Government's downfall. Not only did the miners win, but their victory had far-reaching consequences for the conduct of economic policy by any future Government. By making it plain that, in the field of incomes policy, government had ceased to be the 'authoritative allocator of values for the society' and had become merely one participant, albeit a powerful one, in a complex process of bargaining, the miners' success effectively restricted the range of choices open to government. It greatly increased the probability, for example, that future incomes policies, if they were conducted at all, would be conducted by fiscal rather than direct-interventionist means.

The 1974 miners' strike was thus a major political, even constitutional event. Everyone knew it; no one was surprised by it. Contrast 1974 with 1926. In 1926 the miners were out not for one month but for six; for eight days in May most of the other workers in the country were out too. The 1926 strike did have economic consequences. Half a million men were thrown out of work for a time and valuable coal exports were lost. It also had political consequences. The miners' strike, and in particular the General Strike, led to the passage of the Trade Union and Trade Disputes Act of 1927 and may have contributed to the Conservatives' loss of the

1929 general election. Nevertheless, if the 1926 miners' strike had not been accompanied, somewhat fortuitously, by the General Strike, it would today almost certainly be largely forgotten (except by the miners); its place in history would be small. The Baldwin Government did not fall; on the contrary, its authority, and the authority of government generally, was strengthened. The strike itself 'did not so much end as crumble away'.[4] The miners were forced to accept a reduction in wages.

A full acount of the 1926/1974 contrast would have to allow for a wide variety of factors. For example, the average miner was undoubtedly richer in 1974 than in 1926; this alone strengthened his and his union's bargaining position. But it seems reasonable to argue that the main difference between 1926 and 1974 lay in the increased range of responsibilities placed upon government coupled with the vastly increased number of dependency relationships in which government found itself involved – not only involved but involved in such a way that it was dependent on others, not others on it. On the one hand, the Heath Government's handling of the 1973/74 dispute can be understood only in terms of its determination to maintain Stage III of its incomes policy; but the Baldwin Government did not have an incomes policy and could hardly have conceived of itself as having one. On the other, Britain and British industry by the winter of 1973/74 were dependent on coal in a way that would have been unthinkable fifty years before. Worker and householder alike depended on electricity; electricity depended on coal. Its, and their, dependence on coal might have been reduced by an increase in oil consumption; but Britain was dependent for oil on foreigners whom she could not control and who had just put up their prices. This would have been serious enough in any case but was made even more serious by the fact that, if Britain were to be able to meet the increased cost of oil, she would have to sell more to foreigners or borrow more from them. Either way Britain as a country was dependent on foreigners, and so was British government. Each dependence – on miners, on oil exporters, on foreign importers of British goods, on foreign lenders – reinforced the others. Their cumulative effect was to make the enterprise of government far more difficult to carry on.

The same point can be made more abstractly. Suppose that $A$ is dependent on $B$ for the performance of some action $M$ if he is to achieve goal $X$. Suppose further that there is some non-trivial probability, say of .1, of $B$ failing to perform $M$. The probability of $A$ achieving $X$ remains high at .9. But suppose instead that, for the achievement of $X$, $A$ is dependent not only on $B$ to perform $M$, but on $C$ to perform $N$, on $D$ to perform $O$ and on $E$ to perform $P$. Suppose that the probability of an act of non-performance at each stage remains .1. Since there are now four chances of an act of non-performance occurring instead of one, and since probabilities under these circumstances are multiplied, the probability of $A$ achieving $X$ falls to $.9 \times .9 \times .9 \times .9$, i.e. to roughly .66. $A$ is significantly less likely, other things being equal, to reach his goal.

This paradigm is too simple, of course. If $A$ is dependent on $B$, $C$, $D$ and $E$ for the achievement of $X$, they may be dependent on him for the achievement of $Y$. The dependence may be mutual. $A$ also can seek ways of circumventing those on whom he is dependent, by for example persuading $E$ to perform all of $M$, $N$, $O$ and $P$. All the same, the applications of the paradigm to the real world are obvious. If the Wilson Government of 1974 had depended solely on Mr Len Murray for the maintenance of the Social Contract, the chances of the Social Contract being maintained would have been excellent (though not perfect, since Mr Murray might have decided for some reason that the maintenance of a Labour Government in power was no longer in the trade union movement's interest). But in fact it depended not only on Mr Murray but on the General Council of the Trades Union Congress, on the executives of the various individual unions, on shop stewards and ultimately on the rank and file. It also depended, only slightly less directly, on the foreign exporters of oil and other raw materials. Even if all of these groups had been concerned about the Social Contract and reasonably well disposed towards it, the chance of some (so to speak) 'random' act of non-performance occurring somewhere along the line would have been considerable. Not surprisingly, in the end the policy failed. What was true of government and the Social Contract is true *ex hypothesi* of government and the prevention of crime, government and the energy crisis, government and the balance of trade. In the world of the blind, the one-eyed man is king. In the world of the mutually dependent, no one is king.

We have been discussing what happens when the sheer number of dependency relations in the world increases. Given some probability of the occurrence of acts of non-performance or non-compliance, the probability of a government, or anyone else, getting its way is reduced. But, second, what happens when not only is the absolute number of dependency relations increased but so is the probability of an act of non-compliance in any one of them? The answer is obvious : the chances of non-achievement, of failure are increased even further. If $.9 \times 9. \times .9 \times .9$ yields a success probability of .66, $.5 \times .5 \times .5 \times .5$ (say) yields a success probability of .0625. Even-odds on success in one dependency relationship becomes much less than even-odds in several. Again, it seems clear that the chances of acts of non-compliance occurring in the real world have in fact increased enormously in the past few years. Miners were no more likely not to comply in 1974 than in 1926, but doctors, nurses, dustmen, students, teachers, local government officials, criminals, farmers, sugar producers, oil exporters were much more likely not to. Dependence is thus in the 1970s compounded by nonfeasance. The man dependent on his wife to drive him to work finds increasingly that she refuses to do so. The explanation for this higher incidence of non-compliance lies outside the scope of this chapter. What matters for our purposes is the elemental fact of it.

4.   Physical impossibility, lack of resources and dependence/non-compliance are three reasons why men and women may fail to achieve what they set out to achieve. A fourth possible source of failure is intellectual. A man might fail because he did not know or understand that which he needed to know or understand in order to succeed. A learner-driver, however intelligent, would not get very far if he did not know how to steer or change gears.

That lack of knowledge/understanding is an obstacle to success is easy to prove in the case of learner-drivers, rather harder to prove in the case of politicians. For one thing, politicians are less likely than learner-drivers to admit that they do not know or understand. For another, they may not always know when it is lack of knowledge or understanding that constitutes the obstacle. They may think they understand yet find, when they act, that their actions produce unexpected consequences. A 'touch on the brake', as Chancellors of the Exchequer like to put it, intended to slow down the rate of increase in the level of prices at the cost of some slight increase in the level of unemployment, may substantially increase unemployment without having any discernible effect on prices. A reform of the penal system intended to reduce the prison population by making mandatory the suspension of prison sentences on first offenders may result in an increase in the prison population if magistrates impose heavier sentences on first offenders and the number of recidivists does not decline sufficiently.

Lack of understanding, whether acknowledged or not, has of course been a problem for governments since government began. The Aztecs thought, wrongly, that they could keep their enemies at bay by means of human sacrifice; Ramsay MacDonald thought, wrongly, that a balanced budget was a necessary condition of full employment and would have wanted to balance the budget in 1931 even if foreign bankers had not required him to.[5] Nonetheless, it does appear to be the case that men understand less, and realise that they understand less, now than twenty years ago. There are now

24

few policy areas in which politicians and civil servants are prepared to say confidently, 'Yes, we understand. We know that, if this happens, we must do that.' The world, which twenty years ago seemed, if not always hospitable, at least familiar, no longer seems familiar. Politicians used to decide, or at least believe that they were deciding. In the 1970s they merely grope.

This source of failure and the previous one are almost certainly linked. Mutual dependence and non-compliance have resulted, among other things, in non-comprehension. The world has become not only more complex but more interactive. In the words of Professor LaPorte :

> We are caught somehow in spreading webs of dependence. These networks become increasingly hard to understand. We act, supposing that the consequences of our actions will be acceptable. Yet our actions often prompt reactions unforeseen and unwanted. We seem to have unfamiliar connections to others, connections whose strength and locus change frequently. The duty of comprehension often burdens us uncomfortably . . . [6]

## Consequences

Britain, then, has become harder to govern. The reason it has become harder to govern is that, at one and the same time, the range of problems that government is expected to deal with has vastly increased, and its capacity to deal with problems, even many of the ones it had before, has decreased. It is not the increase in the number of problems alone that matters, or the reduction in capacity. It is the two coming together.

The point is more clearly made if we return to the sugar-shortage example. British Governments are now held responsible for providing the British people with sugar. But supplies of sugar are not now as easy to come by as they once were. In the 1920s and 1930s, Governments were not responsible for providing sugar; but, if they had been, they would not have found it a difficult responsibility to discharge. Ample supplies of sugar were available cheaply (too cheaply from the growers' point of view) on the world market. In the 1970s, Governments are held responsible; but, even so, no one would be very conscious of the fact if sugar in the quantities demanded were readily available. The fact that it is not means, in effect, that government has assumed a new responsibility at the very moment, more or less, when it has ceased to be able to discharge it. That way, in the world of commerce, bankruptcy lies.

What are the consequences for government of a world at once more demanding and more intractable? The main one – that the policies of government more often fail – has already been mentioned. Indeed this was what we have been trying to explain. But three others are worth commenting on briefly.

The first has already been much advertised in politicians' speeches and in the Sunday newspapers : namely, that mass dissatisfaction with the consequences of our present political arrangements could grow to the point where the arrangements themselves were seriously called in question. A system of government, especially a liberal system, is like a bank, in that, to a considerable extent, it relies on confidence. If confidence is lost, there may be a 'run on government' comparable to a run on a bank. The customers may look for new places to lodge their trust. If in addition the leaders of government lose confidence in themselves, the citizen/ customers may rally round whichever leader, if any, has not lost confidence. Although no one has produced a plausible scenario for the collapse of the present British system of government, the fact that people are talking about the possibility at all is in itself significant, and certainly we seem likely in the mid or late 1970s to face the sort of 'crisis of the regime' that Britain has not known since 1832, possibly not since the seventeenth century.

A second possible consequence of governmental 'overload'

26

would be felt first inside the government machine, perhaps to some extent has been already. If the demands are greater, the size of the machine needed to deal with them is likely to be greater. If the problems are more intractable, the machine needed to deal with them is likely to be more complex. Complexity added to scale yields further complexity. It is a fair guess that the number of Whitehall committees, and the number of man and woman hours, devoted to reducing inconsistency and to achieving policy 'coherence' is vastly greater than it was twenty years ago. The creation of the Central Policy Review Staff and of Mr Harold Wilson's 'policy unit' at 10 Downing Street have been described as efforts to augment the power of the prime minister. To an outsider both look more like rather desperate attempts to cope with complexity. If British government seems even less assertive and more reactive than in the past, if ministers seem even more overworked, if 'accidents' – blowings off course – seem even more frequent, if the short term constantly gets the better of the long, the phenomena we have been discussing seem likely to constitute part of the explanation.

A third possible consequence of these same phenomena would be a quite radical change in the nature of government, and in our conceptions of it. The idea is deeply embedded in the minds of most citizens, and even of most political scientists, that somehow, sooner or later 'the Government will decide'. The Government is authoritative. 'They' will deal with it. We yield enormous powers to government in theory even while denying them in practice. In fact, it seems probable that the state in Britain, and quite possibly in other Western countries, will have become by the late 1970s, to an even greater extent than now, merely one among a number of contenders for wealth, power and influence, the others including large companies, trade unions and their members, foreign companies, foreign governments, international organisations. In other words, the experience of incomes policy may repeat itself in other fields. If it does, we may find ourselves looking for our models of politics not to Bismarckian Germany or even to the Britain of 1945 but to England before Wolsey, France before Richelieu.

## What is to be done?

However that may be, the combination of increasing demands on government and government's increasing inability to cope seems certain to produce consequences of some sort, and most of us are probably uneasily aware that they could be unpleasant. One does not have to be a doom-monger to sense that something is wrong with our polity as well as our economy. If overload is a bad thing, what, if anything, can be done about it?

In principle, one could tackle the problem on the demands/expectations/responsibilities side or on the failure/intractability side. One could try either to decrease government's reach or to increase its grasp. In practice, there does not seem to be much to be looked for on the failure/intractability side. Dependency relations are not likely to become less frequent in the future; rather the reverse. Acts of non-compliance are likewise unlikely to become less frequent. Our understanding of social complexity will undoubtedly increase, but not necessarily faster than the growth of complexity itself. We shall probably have to run very hard, intellectually, to stay in the same place.

We have, therefore, to look to the demands/expectations side. 'Government,' said Burke, 'is a contrivance of human wisdom to provide for human wants.' Wisdom and the ability to provide for wants being in short supply, it seems prudent to try to reduce the incidence of wants, or at least of wants-of-government. How? It is disconcerting that the suggestions that come to mind are almost boy-scoutish in their banality – and in their dependence on good will and on long-term rather than immediate self-interest. One possibility might be to try again, as it were, to make Herbert Morrison stick : to remove some of the functions of government from the purview of the politically-elected Government and to persuade politicians, in their own long-term self-interest, to agree that such functions, once removed, should not be un-removed. But this seems a forlorn hope. The experiences of the nationalised industries and of the 1970–74 Heath Government both suggest that it is almost impossible in a competitive democracy to make the political non-political or prevent the potentially political from becoming actually so.

Even a change of style – in which politicians ceased to claim that they alone knew how to solve the country's problems, and ceased to blame other politicians quite so enthusiastically for failing to solve them – would be very hard to achieve in circumstances of electoral competition, though it must be said that the leaders of all of the major parties have already adopted a tone somewhat more humble than in the past. The most that can be hoped for is probably a marginal reduction in the work load of ministers by devolving onto other authorities some of the more routine elements of public administration and by abandoning formally the doctrine that the minister is personally responsible for everything that happens in his or her department. This sort of unrealism anyway only encourages unrealism about government in general.

It is hard not to be a little pessimistic about the future. Governments have tried to play God. They have failed. But they go on trying. How can they be made to stop? Academic political scientists have traditionally been concerned to improve the performance of government. Perhaps over the next few years they should be more concerned with how the number of tasks that government has come to be expected to perform can be reduced.

# NOTES

This chapter is a slightly revised version of an article that first appeared in the special 1950–1975 anniversary number of *Political Studies* 23 (1975), 284–96. Published by Oxford University Press.

1  On the subject of popular expectations of government, see also Samuel Brittan's chapter in this book. Brittan's chapter and this one are complementary in many ways.

2  The book was published in 1933 by Constable. The quotations below are drawn from pages 141 and 272.

3  On the idea of increased interdependence and its consequences, which are still only just beginning to be appreciated, see Todd LaPorte, ed., *Organized Social Complexity: Challenge to Politics and Policy* (Princeton, N.J.: Princeton University Press, 1975). Professor LaPorte was kind enough to let me see the typescript of this book and I have benefited greatly from conversations with him. His treatment of this whole subject is more formal and more rigorous than mine.

4  Charles Loch Mowat, *Britain between the Wars, 1918–1940* (London: Methuen, 1955), p. 334. It is interesting that all of the standard histories of the inter-war period concentrate on the General Strike rather than the miners' strike. They say almost nothing about the 'political economy' of the miners' strike. For example, they say nothing about the size of coal stocks at the beginning of the strike.

5  An excellent case-study of the influence of abstract ideas on the conduct of public policy is Robert Skidelsky, *Politicians and the Slump* (London: Macmillan, 1967).

6  LaPorte, *Organized Social Complexity,* Chap. 1.

# Politicians and the sorcerer: the problems of governing with capitalism in crisis

David Coates

The fact that we can seriously discuss whether Britain is becoming more difficult to govern is itself a measure of how rapidly and radically the national political scene has changed. This was not the kind of question suggested by even a passing acquaintance with British political life in the 1950s and early 1960s. Then political parties that were divided by only minute differences of priority and policy presided over an apparently stable world of slow but steady economic growth, near full employment and persistently rising living standards. It was a world acceptable to all major shades of political opinion, in which economic management by any Government was an essential and relatively uncontroversial element. The daily content of political debate was largely technical, turning on how commonly accepted social and economic issues were to be resolved. Rarely if ever did public debate in those years focus on whether political issues could be resolved at all, or on whether their resolution did not in fact require radical changes in the structures of ownership and control in a modern industrial society. In 'an age of affluence' politics was about the solving of problems, and an atmosphere of optimism and official consensus prevailed on the definition of problems and solutions alike.

But now things have changed. Politicians seem less certain of their ability to govern and to lead, and the gap between promises made in opposition and performance in office is widening again for both the Conservatives and Labour. We are now all too familiar with the reversal in economic and social policy that invariably seems to come after a year or two in power. Indeed, politicians now face problems that would have been inconceivable in the 1950s : persistent and enormous balance of payments deficits, large-scale currency movements and a depreciating pound; generalised inflation and at the same time high and growing levels of unemployment; falling national production and cutbacks in the growth rate of public spending, which eat away at plans for social reform and welfare provision; and growing trade union militancy that is capable of thwarting legislative initiatives and of destroying the credibility of Governments for foreign financiers and electors alike.

It is little wonder that new elements are entering the language in which the political scene is descri' ed. The repeated call for greater industrial efficiency, cost-effectiveness and increased exports is now linked to warnings of national crisis and to appeals for national regeneration. If Prime Ministers, Chancellors, editors and business leaders are to be believed, it is not that Britain is simply becoming more difficult to govern. It is rather that, in the critical area of industrial and economic policy, the difficulty is to govern at all. I want in this chapter to try and show why this is so.

## Explanations of the current crisis

There are many explanations of the current state of British political and economic life, each carrying with it an allocation of responsibility and a set of recommendations for action. Many people are prepared to argue that the responsibility for any current difficulties lies firmly in our existing political institutions and processes. They claim that politicians are no longer of a sufficiently high moral and intellectual calibre to inspire national unity in time of crisis. We are told that political debate itself undermines confidence in any of the contending parties. Or the machinery of government, and the civil servants who run it, are said to lack the experience in industry and the technocratic skills that are thought vital for an age in which Governments, under heavy electoral pressure, are drawn more and more into the planning and direction of economic affairs. Even the present electoral arrangements, with their bias against small nationally-spread parties, have been criticised for stultifying party competition, for disenfranchising large groups of electors, and for giving a monopoly of political office to parties whose disproportionate dependence on either business or the trade unions leaves them insufficiently independent to establish permanent co-operation between workers and managements.

Other possibly more familiar explanations go beyond political institutions to link the present crisis to defects in the distribution of power and effort in industry and commerce. This is surely where the differences of opinion among Right, Centre and Left in British political life are most obvious, with all but the Left prone to argue that things would be much better but for the power of trade unions, the irresponsibility of trade-union leadership, and the widespread persistence of restrictive and inefficient labour practices in industry. Arguing against all this, the left wing of the Labour party have explained their government's present difficulties by linking the low rate of investment in manufacturing plant and equipment to the lack of public ownership, to the absence of democratic state planning, and to the machinations of private ownership and the City. Instead of blaming workers and their unions, the Labour Left has tended to stress the low quality of senior management, and the restricted social background from which so many senior executives and directors come, as major reasons for the poor performance of British industry in the world market.

Or, if none of this is to your liking, then there are still those explanations which single out foreign conspirators as the cause of our national downfall, whether these are oil sheiks, ruthless Zurich speculators, bureaucrats from Brussels or Moscow-trained communist agitators. Alternatively, everything can be related to the loss of Empire, or to that supposedly general fall in moral standards in a too affluent, too secular and too pornographic world, which is certainly in need of a rekindling of the Dunkirk spirit, if not of a Festival of Light. If the number of explanations available provided the key to a solution, national recovery would have happened long ago. But the key, of course, is quality of explanation rather than quantity – and there the story is rather different.

I want to argue that the only way in which the present political situation can be fully understood is in terms of a crisis generated by capitalism, and that the ultimate reason for the inadequacy of all the explanations listed above is their failure to recognise this. To persuade you of this it will be necessary to explain what I mean by 'capitalism' and to try and show the force of a Marxist explanation of our situation. But first let me make some comments on the alternative explanations that I have laid out.

Some will not do at all. There is little conclusive evidence of any marked decline in the quality of our political leadership, though the widespread belief that there has been tells us much about the way we choose to remember our political history. Certainly the aristocratic background of politicians is less in evidence than it was up to 1945. But that might be counted a desirable change, and certainly the quality of political leadership between the wars is not something to which any of us would want to return. Nor is there overwhelming evidence that what we face is a 'machinery of government' problem or one that cries out for civil service or electoral reform. The civil service is in need of reform for other reasons, and the machinery of government is often under heavy pressure. But the problems that governments face are those of their relationship to private concentrations of power and to wider social processes. If the internal organisation and personnel of the Government's machine, or its electoral base, affect that relationship, they do so only at the margin; and Governments will still find that it is difficult to implement their policies in industrial and economic fields long after the completion of any civil service reform or departmental reorganisation, and no matter by which electoral system they have been elected into office.

It is because the problem of 'governability' turns ultimately on relationships between ministers and the world of industry, finance and labour that the arguments about trade-union power, restrictive practices and the role of the City carry so much more weight. They pull us in the right direction, but they do not tell us enough, and in stopping where they do they obscure the actual processes of power and influence at work. If trade-union power is a problem, we still have to ask why trade unions now feel it necessary to pitch their demands so high, why their demands should bring them into conflict with Governments, and why trade-union leaders should now find themselves regularly trapped between a militant membership and a government with which they wish to avoid conflict. We have to ask, too, why restrictive practices should be retained so tenaciously, and why this should be of increasing concern to ministers as well as to industrialists. We need to know why investment in new manufacturing plant is so low and why foreign financiers are suddenly so powerful. It would also be useful to be able to suggest why so many explanations are offered that do not touch on these questions at all or do not deal with them satisfactorily. To do all these things it is essential to see the mounting problems faced by politicians in a wider capitalist context. This task will take us away, for a moment, from the immediate problems of government, to an examination of the society which Governments attempt to shape and control.

## Inequality in a class society

Perhaps the first thing to say of our society is that it is divided by class. However often we are told that a certain job is more important than another, or is more skilled, or carries more responsibility and the like, we should never forget that the production of the goods and services on which our way of life (indeed our very existence) depends involves each and every one of us playing a part. Production is a collective act to which, directly or indirectly, now or in the future, all of us are essential. And yet the goods and services that we produce collectively, and the social power and prestige that we generate, are not divided equally among us. Rather our access to goods, services, power and prestige differs with the position in the class structure into which we were born, or into which (for a surprisingly small number of us) we move.

Think of how our society has built up a wages system with its own arbitrary logic, by which some jobs are rewarded to a greater degree than others, with no regard to the actual needs of the men and women who perform them. It is still fair to say that there is a tendency within this society for groups of workers who experience the most adverse working conditions to earn less than other groups whose work is less demanding and more secure. If that sounds unreasonable, consider which groups of workers are most likely to work regular shifts, to begin work earliest in the morning, to experience accidents at work or to suffer from industrially-induced diseases, which are most prone to short-time working and to unemployment, and most likely to experience falling real earnings as they enter their 50s and poverty after 65. The answer, surely, when all the exceptions have been conceded, is that these crucial features of industrial life are much more the lot of unskilled and semi-skilled manual workers than of their managerial or professional counterparts. Even the much maligned 'affluent' car worker has to work longer hours in worse conditions, subject to the monotony and pressure of the moving production line, to take home an income that is commonplace amongst the managerial and professional class. We are not a society of equals in the world of work, and as a result Governments should not be surprised that they repeatedly fail to find any automatic and long-lasting harmony of interests among different occupational groups when they attempt to implement policy on industrial relations and the growth of incomes.

We are not a society of equals in consumption and leisure either. The inequalities here correspond closely with those at work, from which they largely derive, and compound the potential and actual differences of interests between classes which gives so hollow a ring to the repeated call of Governments for unity 'in the national interest'. People's access to the products of their common act of productive labour – housing, consumer goods, education, social services, cultural facilities, even to health itself – reflects the class-controlled distribution of wealth and income that has been transmitted to this generation from the past. It is true that general standards of consumption, health and welfare have risen steadily from the 1930s, but the inequalities of distribution remain. Wealth remains heavily concentrated in the hands of a few – those who have benefited from the accumulation of capital and the ownership of land by earlier generations of their families, while at the other extreme, to quote Roy Jenkins, 'the total of all those whose incomes is below, at or a little above Supplementary Benefit scale level is 10.6 million'.[1] This is one in five of the population. John Westergaard summed it up well when he wrote that there is a

class structured pattern of inequality in economy and society at large. All workers, manual and increasingly the routine non-manual, are vulnerable : liable to the hazards of poverty or near poverty in old age, in sickness, on a change of family circumstances, on redundancy or short time, in the later years of working life. Their vulnerability even in 'affluence' is quite different from the security which characterises middle and upper class life cycles, and which derives, not only from higher incomes, but from career patterns with cumulative increments, promotion prospects and fringe benefits, from possession or likelihood of inheritance of property, even on a limited scale; from material or other aid often available at critical points from relations; from easier access to and affinity in communication with, the supporting institutions of everyday life – educational, legal, social, administrative and health services.[2]

Behind this lies a dimension of social power. We are not a totalitarian state, nor a dictatorship, and democratic liberties count for much. But the recognition of our democratic freedoms should not be allowed to obscure from view the heavy concentration of power that lies behind them. The right to initiate the majority of the rules under which we live, the predominant influence over the ideas and opinions to which we are regularly exposed, and the ultimate control of the forms of coercion to which we are subject, are all in the hands of a relatively small group of men. These men either own or control (or share similar social backgrounds and identifications with those who own and control) the means of production, distribution and exchange in a complex capitalist economy. Although as a class they are often divided internally on many issues, they are nonetheless capable of showing a truly remarkable degree of unanimity and resolve in crisis or under challenge. They are the group of men which Governments find it particularly difficult to control, and whom in only a limited sense can Governments be said to 'govern' at all.[3]

Of course it is true that the precise impact of these inequalities of industrial experience, material reward and social prestige are moderated by the degree of organisation and militancy displayed by institutions created or sustained by the working class (into which social grouping must now increasingly be included the growing body of routine white-collar workers). But the allocation of social rewards and power against which trade unions struggle is neither random nor accidental, nor is it one governed by principles of human need or by the genetically-transmitted distribution of aptitudes and skills between individuals or groups. Rather trade unions and workers find that some men, and only some men, are in a position to monopolise a disproportionately large share of the social product, and to transmit the advantages

38

of their class position more or less easily to their children. They can do this because they successfully lay claim to the ownership of the machinery and the products of the collective acts of labour, and because they occupy positions of command within the central owning institutions of contemporary capitalism (that is, in the multi-national corporations, the joint-stock companies, the finance houses and the public corporations that dominate production in our society). Similarly it is because the majority of men and women do not own either the tools with which they work, or the products of their collective act of labour, and because they occupy subordinate positions in the bureaucracies of capitalism, that they experience a different and more limited set of life chances. And it is because the working class occupy the lowest position in these bureaucracies that their experience of the instabilities and inequalities of such a social order are so extreme. It is this tenacious and class-based inequality that Governments face – with the radically different life styles and interests that it necessarily produces – that is the first key to any fully adequate explanation of why Britain is becoming so difficult to govern.

But of itself this is not enough. Such a stable and persistent pattern of class inequalities can offer a clue to why Government appeals for national unity tend to fail, and it certainly suggests that Governments are being either stupid or disingenuous when they deny the actual bias of their policies against some groups in favour of others. What it cannot do is explain why, in the 1970s, governing has suddenly become so much more difficult. To handle that problem we need to look too at the processes at work on this structure of class-based inequalities. We need to look, that is, at what is specifically 'capitalist' about it.

## The instability of capitalism

What then is 'capitalism'? The question is easier to put than to answer, not least because of the disagreements that have attended the meaning of the term. For some the term has been synonymous with industrialism in general, for others only with industrialism's nineteenth-century variant, long since passed. For a major German sociologist like Max Weber, what has made a society 'capitalist' has been the predominance within it of the systematic pursuit of profit within stable bureaucratic economic and political organisations.[4] For Marxists however, and it is in their sense that the term is being used here, capitalism is to be understood as a society whose system of production is characterised by two main features. First, the production of wealth is carried out by wage labourers – men and women who sell their labour power to others in return for money wages. These wage labourers do not own the goods and services that they produce. Nor do they own the tools or machinery with which they work. All that they own is their labour power, and to survive they have to sell that to other men, who own the machinery of production and distribution and who successfully lay claim to the ownership of all that is produced by the labourers they employ. This latter class of men – the capitalist bourgeoisie – create and maintain their social position in two ways : first by requiring their employees to perform surplus labour (that is, to go on working for longer that is necessary merely to meet their own needs); and then by realising, as their profit, the additional value created in those extra hours through the sale in the world market of the total goods and services that their labour force has produced. Capitalism, that is, is not simply based on wage labour. Its second main feature is that is is also a system of production in which goods are produced, not for immediate consumption by the producers, but for exchange; as a result, it is a system in which the criteria that govern production are not those of immediate human needs but are rather those of profit-making and capital accumulation through exchange and trade. In both of these respects, capitalism differs from the feudal society that preceded it, where production predominantly based on a subsistence agriculture, with only a limited exchange of surpluses between the countryside and the small guild manufacturers of the emerging urban centres.

The main point to be grasped if we are fully to understand why Britain is becoming so difficult to govern is that the capitalist system under which we live is a relatively recent form of social organisation and production. The history of Western Europe since the Middle Ages has been dominated by its emergence, through the transformation of a feudal peasantry into an urban-based industrial labour force, and by the associated rise to social and political power of a body of capitalist entrepreneurs who were able, from the surpluses created by the labour they employed, to accumulate the vast concentrations of industrial plant and machinery, and the financial capital, on which the present industrial system rests. As Marx said,

> Owners of money or owners of commodities, on the one hand, and persons who own nothing but their labour power, on the other, are not natural products. The relation has not a natural basis, nor is it one met with in all historical epochs. It is manifestly the outcome of an antecedent historical evolution, the product of numerous economic transformations, the upshot of the decay of a whole series of older forms of social production.[5]

The world has not always been capitalist, and governing it is difficult to a very large extent only because it is.

For from the outset this capitalist system of production has been uniquely unstable and prone to crisis. True, there have been periods lately in which that instability has been damped down, and in which Governments have come to believe that they could control, and even remove, the propensity of the economic system to periodically overproduce, resulting in workers laid off and plants left idle. But we are discovering again now that the optimism of Keynesian economics was misplaced, and that there is still an inherent long term tendency in capitalist production for the rate of profit to fall. The explanation of this tendency, as Marx explained in

Volume III of *Capital*, lies in capitalism's propensity to replace men (the source of value, and hence profit in the system) by machines; and it is this that gives to the kind of social and economic order under which we live a central instability which no Government can totally eradicate, however hard it tries. Its major immediate consequence is the perpetual re-creation of the tension between capitalist and worker, as workers unite to resist their employer's repeated attempts to intensify and/or extend the period of their work, so as to increase the productivity of their labour, which is the main strategy available to him in his attempt to offset this erosion of his rate of profit. The falling profit rate also inspires (and is then intensified by) competition between capitalists, and extends that competition onto a world scale, as new markets are sought and still more productive machinery is introduced, to compensate for the falling rate of return on previous investment in existing markets. A new market, or a new technology, provides for the individual capitalist some temporary respite from the pressure on profits, but one that is only temporary, as the new markets are invaded by competitors and as successful technological innovations are first copied and then superseded. In the periodic crises of overproduction that accompany these competitive struggles, small companies are inevitably destroyed, leaving the fight against the erosion of profit rates in the next period in the hands of fewer and larger companies. It is in this way that under capitalism we are left with a system of production in which frenetic competition and a desperate search for corporate profits goes on at a steadily higher level of investment, dependent on an ever higher level of demand, but with in the end a declining rate of profits for the capitalist class as a whole. As Marx said in 1848,

> the bourgeoisie cannot exist without constantly revolutionising the instruments of production, and thereby the relations of production, and with them the whole relations of society. Conservation of the old modes of produc-

tion in unaltered form was, on the contrary, the first condition of existence for all earlier industrial classes. Constant revolutionising of production, uninterrupted disturbance of all social conditions, everlasting uncertainty and agitation distinguish the bourgeois epoch from all earlier ones . . . Modern bourgeois society . . . is like the sorcerer who is no longer able to control the powers of the nether world whom he has called up by his spells.[6]

This is still true; and what Governments have to cope with is the financial and economic dislocation, and at times with the crises, that it produces.

Of course Marx seriously underestimated capitalism's capacity to sustain itself, to survive its crises, and we would be foolish to do the same. At certain moments, when the self-destructive tendencies of capitalist production have been masked, by increased labour productivity or by the development of new markets for example, Western Europe has known periods of relatively steady economic growth and prosperity. We have just lived through one such period. Britain is becoming more difficult to govern now because that period of steady growth appears to be over. The old instabilities of intensifying competition and falling profits have been joined by widespread price inflation to throw Governments into difficulties and sections of the labour movement into militancy. It is the reappearance of marked instability in the international capitalist system that is the backcloth against which the specific features of Britain's political difficulties in the 1970s must be seen.

## The weakness of British capitalism

Several features of Western capitalism since the late 1950s are particularly significant for any specification of the problems currently faced by British politicians. The first is the accelerated concentration in the ownership and control of the means of production that has occurred in the last fifteen years. Clearly some industries have long been dominated by a few large firms, but the scale and character of industrial mergers has changed of late. Between 1967 and 1970 'perhaps around one-fifth of all assets of industrial and commercial companies was acquired by other companies',[7] so that one-third of all of the top hundred companies in 1957, and almost a half of the top two thousand, had vanished by 1970.[8] Of those that remain, the larger ones are increasingly multi-national in the scale of their operations and in their ownership. Foreign investment in British industry reached new heights in the 1960s as the giant American combines entered European markets and production points. Foreign-based multinational companies now dominate production in a long list of major industries, so that even as early as 1966 American-owned firms in Britain owned 7.2 per cent of the net capital stock of companies, and were responsible for 17.5 per cent of manufactured exports.[9] This concentration and shift in industrial ownership went hand in hand with the growth and intensification of international competition. Between 1954 and 1970 British-based firms lost half of their share of the world market in manufactured goods. This rate of decline in the share of the world market was particularly marked after 1964, and was mirrored by an increase in international competition in the domestic market as well. Between 1958 and 1968 the volume of imported manufactured goods increased almost four-fold, so that, whereas only 8 per cent of all imported manufactured goods consumed were imported in 1956, by 1970 that figure was 15 per cent.[10]

The fact that British firms did so badly as international competition increased, and were vulnerable to the influxes of foreign capital that Governments find so difficult to control, illustrates the particular weakness of British capitalism in the 1960s and 1970s. From the 1950s onwards the national growth rate has lagged behind that of any of the other major capitalist economies. The percentage of the Gross National Product invested in new machinery and industrial plant has remained stubbornly low. The City has continued to act as a channel for the export of capital, and indeed carried out a long rearguard action through the 1960s against any devaluation of the pound. Patterns of trade have been slow to break from a preoccupation with Imperial and Commonwealth markets that were growing less rapidly than world trade as a whole in the 1950s and 1960s. And, with a significance that we shall discuss later, the trade unions have remained strongly entrenched. As early as 1961 Governments found themselves presiding over an economy that was insufficiently competitive to prevent repeated and ever more serious balance of payments crises which through the 1960s forced ministers of both parties to impose deflationary policies that still further eroded future levels of investment and sales. By 1968–70 the Labour Government faced a widespread collapse in profits in many sections of British manufacturing industry.[11] In the 1970s this was exacerbated by widespread inflation, itself mainly the product of the very Government policies that Keynesian economists and Labour party politicians had been advocating for so long as *the* way of solving capitalist instability and British competitive weakness.[12] It was this systemically-induced inflation, and the world-wide recession into which the capitalist economies were moving by 1974–75, which the political instabilities of the Middle East intensified and to which the recent large trade-union wage demands have been an understandable defensive response.[13]

The significance of all this for the development of British politics cannot be overstated. The weakness of British capitalism now dominates political life at every turn. To 'strengthen the economy' has become the key promise of every aspiring Government. After the general retreat from detailed intervention in industrial affairs in the 1950s, policies of late have responded increasingly to the demands for assistance that have emerged from industrial leaders and pressure group spokesmen. These demands have fallen into a particular pattern. Around 1960 what was then the Federation of British Industries began to press for government help in indicative planning, to provide a stable framework of expectations within which investment could be organised far in advance. Throughout the 1960s and 1970s requests came from firms in particularly acute commercial difficulties for government credits to save jobs and to prevent any loss of national production. Increasingly, as international competition grew and intensified, Governments also came under heavy pressure to control wages, to increase the productivity of labour, and to take the pressure of organised groups of workers off already heavily-squeezed profit margins. In this last respect at least, the weakness of British capitalism in our period led Governments to make a sharp break with their traditional peacetime practice of leaving industrial relations and collective bargaining in the private sector well and truly alone.

This demand for government action against organised labour connects with one last aspect of why Britain is becoming more difficult to govern : namely the strength and growing militancy of the trade-union movement. It is clearly dangerous to generalise on the industrial experience of over 24,000,000 working people, though possibly generalisations are more valid now than in the early 1950s because of the growing impact on all of us of recent government policies on income restraint, productivity bargaining and industrial relations reform. Yet there are discernible patterns in British industrial relations since the 1950s, patterns that indicate the impact of the growing weakness of British capitalism on the workers who produce its wealth, and the increasing involvement of Governments in their attempts to replace that weakness with a high rate of economic growth, a strong pound sterling, a favourable balance of payments and a higher level of investment in manufacturing plant.

Certainly we can distinguish between the industrial experience of two broad groups of workers in British industry since the mid 1950s. One group, including miners, textile workers and railwaymen, spent large parts of the period in contracting industries. They were part of a declining labour force, who saw their industries run down and found themselves, until recently, in a weak bargaining position, slipping further and further down the earnings table. The majority of these workers were employed in the public sector, and experienced government policies towards their industries, as well as on the wider issues of pay and conditions, as a major obstacle to any attempt they might make to transform an industrial situation dominated by low pay and depressed working conditions. By the late 1950s it began to appear that workers' resistance to this run-down of their industries would be minimal, and Governments were able to implement incomes policy norms without fear of major confrontation. Throughout the public sector, these norms were applied tightly in the 1960s as an example to private employers who tended to be more lax. It was this decade of discrimination against workers who were invariably amongst the lowest paid anyway that generated from 1969 onwards the resentment and militancy that has not so far abated.

This industrial experience was quite different from that of the skilled and semi-skilled manual workers in the crucial growth and export manufacturing sectors – in chemicals, in light engineering, in motor vehicles and in the docks. The high level of demand for the products of these industries, the absence of sustained competition until the 1960s, and the general scarcity of skilled labour combined to strengthen the position of local work groups and their shop stewards against both management and national union officials. The result was the creation of what the Donovan Commission in 1968 called a two-tier system of collective bargaining, in which nationally negotiated wage rates were increased considerably at factory or shop level by the negotiation of extra bonuses, piece-rates and overtime payments. The resulting wage drift was buttressed by a pattern of short, small and normally unofficial strikes, which enabled groups of workers to extend their control into a number of crucial aspects of their work situation. Though the position clearly varied between factories, there does appear to have been a general tendency

47

across the engineering industries in the late 1950s and 1960s for workers to have a considerable influence over the allocation of overtime, the level and flexibility of manning and the pace of work, over shift work, and even at times over questions of discipline and dismissal.[14] It is understandable that, when all this was challenged by Government policy after 1964, workers in these industries fought to hold onto the income levels, and the degree of control over their own work situation, that they had achieved.

The crisis in competitiveness and profits that hit British capitalism in the 1960s brought Governments into increasing conflict with well-organised sections of the labour movement, even when those Governments were Labour Governments, dependent on working-class votes. In a very real sense no Government had much choice. It did not make the world it was trying to control, and the continuity of that world was more than enough to ensure a marked similarity in policy between Governments of supposedly different political persuasions. Any Government was under heavy pressure from business leaders for assistance in controlling wage costs and increasing productivity, in order to strengthen the competitive position and the profit levels of industry. Henry Ford even arrived in person, you may remember, to tell Edward Heath this, and to persuade the Government to mend its ways if it wanted to see any more of his company's investments. Governments were even more tightly constrained by the balance of payment deficits created by the lack of competitiveness, for foreign loans were available only on terms that insisted on increasingly strong Government action against wage drift, industrial militancy and so-called restrictive practices. And Governments were pulled in the same direction by their own interventionist propensities, and by their need for higher productivity if their policies of social reform were to be funded without creating inflation. Even before spiralling prices added their own imperative, both Labour and Conservative Cabinets found themselves drawn into a more regular involvement in the problems of industrial and labour management, with all the pitfalls this could involve when that management clashed with the interests of well-placed groups of workers and their union officials.

Policy here has gone through a number of stages. In the early 1960s the emphasis was on voluntarily-based incomes policies to curb wage drift; and in the first months of the Labour Government of 1964 national union leaders were persuaded to agree to keep wage settlements within the bounds set by the growth rate of national productivity. This agreement was enough to set in motion those tight pay negotiations in the public sector that by 1969 had built up militancy among groups like teachers, firemen and local government manual workers who had no tradition of industrial action. But it was ineffective in the manufacturing sector, where local rather than national agreements were the basis of wage drift. Rapidly realising what was happening, a Labour Government under heavy foreign pressure quickly switched its emphasis onto productivity-bargaining within the context of a statutorily-based incomes policy, allowing pay settlements above the norm only where workers accepted more 'strenuous' working conditions. Intriguingly, the conditions specified by successive White Papers as constituting a more strenuous work routine covered precisely those aspects of the work situation over which groups of workers had established some degree of control in the 1950s. A productivity agreement was held to be acceptable within the policy if workers surrendered restrictive practices (that is, their control) over the allocation of overtime or shift work, if they allowed flexibility of manning on machines, if they replaced piece-work payment systems by measured day work, or if they allowed manning levels to fall. Six million workers signed such agreements between 1966 and 1969, yet still the crisis of profits and competitiveness grew more severe. For many agreements were bogus, and too many that were not were eroded as workers refused to sign their second and third stages. So, doubtless reluctantly, Labour ministers allowed unemployment to rise, and later both Labour and Conservative Governments attempted to introduce legal restrictions on certain kinds of trade-union and worker activity. In the case of the Conservative Government, this involved the banning of the very tactics by which well-organised work groups had defended their industrial power and their unofficial leadership – that is, short unofficial strikes in breach of grievance procedures, sympathy strikes and the blacking of goods. When that legal initiative also failed, in the face of the dockers' strike and a threatened general strike by the TUC, Conservative and Labour Governments in the last three years have returned to more complex incomes policies, from which the Conservatives at least had claimed to have broken for ever. It is this sharp reversal of policy by both parties, and the repeated failure of public policy to generate sustained growth and competitiveness, that lies behind so much of the current disquiet about the ability of Governments to govern.

But that inability should no longer be surprising. The tasks that Governments set themselves involve nothing less than correcting the weaknesses of investment, competition and profits that are endemic to capitalist production. This would be hard enough without trade union militancy, but militancy is not likely to go away. The very crisis that necessitates strong Government action also generates the conditions for militancy against it. Workers experience falling competitiveness, and the low profits and inflation that this brings, as threats to their living standards, their work routines and their jobs. When capitalism is in crisis, they face speed-ups and redundancy. When Governments try to 'solve' the crisis, they add to these dangers of speed-ups, declining living standards and unemployment by the policies they introduce. It is no wonder that trade unionists object. What is amazing is that their opposition is so muted and so sporadic. Governments will not be able to legislate away either falling rates of profit or competition. Nor will they easily ban worker alienation and militancy. Politics in the future will continue to be dominated by the struggle between a weak capitalism and a militant labour force, and that is going to make the job of a practising politician particularly difficult and unrewarding.

## Political alternatives

I hope that it is clear by now why I am so unhappy with the alternative explanations of the current situation discussed earlier. Governments are overloaded not mainly because of electoral demands, but because of the pressures created by the crisis in the productive system that surrounds them. No strong political or industrial leadership can talk the crisis away and 'responsibility' in trade-union leadership would be less a solution than a stage in driving militancy into unofficial hands. An attack on 'idleness' and 'restrictive practices' will ease the pressure for as long as it can be maintained, but only at the price of intensifying the work routines of an already intensely-worked and alienated labour force. Nor will conspiracy theories help us to a true understanding of our situation. The Communist party has not had the impact on industrial relations that its supporters, and the right-wing press, would have us think it has had. Industrial militancy now involves too many people, and too serious a set of issues, to be dismissed as the work of a handful of 'misguided and mischievous' people. Nor are most foreign holders of sterling balances merely idle speculators gambling for quick returns at the nation's expense. Among the major holders of foreign currency are multinational corporations and finance houses driven by the weakness of British capitalism to move their money out of sterling in order to maintain their profit levels in a world of uncertain exchange rates. The job of governing Britain is difficult because Governments find themselves constrained, as they have always been, by the concentrations of power in business, finance and labour. It is becoming more difficult now because, amid those concentrations of power, the need to accumulate capital and to maintain profits is setting up ever sharper tensions between capitalist and capitalist, and between capitalist and worker.

Indeed, so far as the trade-union movement is concerned, Governments now face only a limited range of alternative policies. They can call again for voluntary pay restraint and for co-operation in the 'streamlining' of production. But, as the 1960s showed, such a voluntary call is difficult to sustain. It works, if it works at all, only when Governments can declare that a 'crisis' is upon us, and indeed this is doubtless one of the reasons why we are told so often that one is. But the very permanence of Government involvement in incomes policy and industrial relations makes that kind of appeal less and less effective, and runs the risk of merely culminating in a wages 'explosion' when the specified period of restraint is over. That is presumably one of the reasons for the Conservative party's decision to use legislative changes of a different kind, with their attempt to ban certain of the forms of behaviour and organisation that workers characteristically use in the pursuit of wage demands and control over their work situation. The difficulty that the Conservative Government experienced will presumably dissuade others from trying again in quite the same way. But the underlying rationale of the policy – the strengthening of official trade union structures against unofficial action and independent shop floor organisation – will surely continue to be one plank of Government policy.

What the Labour Government found with its 'social contract' was that its middle way between voluntarism and compulsion itself broke down. The logic of the argument behind the 'contract' was clear : that no voluntary policy of wage restraint could last long while the structure of inequalities discussed earlier persisted. But already the Labour Government has found that in so weak a competitive position, and with inflation running at such a rate, British capitalism cannot afford to see the 'fundamental and irreversible shift in the balance of power and wealth in favour of working people and their families' promised by the Labour Party's *Programme* in 1973.[15] On the contrary, a strengthening of the economy's competitive position, and a diminution in the rate of inflation, require a slight intensification of the inequalities already in existence. Wealth, income and power have to be moved away from labour and the working class towards capital and the managerial class. Progressive taxation cannot be increased without reducing still further domestic levels of saving and investment. Social services and welfare benefits cannot be increased on the scale promised without inflation rates rocketing even higher. Under pressure from its own left wing, the Labour Government is currently exploring how severely the crisis that it faces will cut into its programme. The Labour Left is still convinced that an alternative set of Government policies is possible and attainable, if only there is the political will and the electoral support. I have argued elsewhere my doubts about this.[16] As far as I can tell, the thinking of the Labour Left has not yet grasped the crucial extent to which public spending under capitalism is itself a major cause of inflation, and how – as a result – the majority of the planned reforms in welfare, income re-distribution and power sharing will fall victim to the Government's prior commitment to price stability.

This Labour Government seems set on a path whose components we have seen before. An incomes policy norm has now been specified, and the legislative and coercive powers of the Government machine are to be used against recalcitrant employers and through them against trade unionists seeking to avoid cuts in their living standards and job security. Unemployment will be allowed to rise, which will help to reduce some of the bargaining power of militant workers. A major campaign of publicity is already under way, stressing the need for national restraint in an attempt to reduce rank-and-file trade-union pressure for greater wage settlements and job control. In addition, trade-union leaders are continually urged to pull their own unions behind the

Government's policies of retrenchment and unemployment, in the name of a wider national interest that is actually hard to locate in so divided and so capitalist a society. In fact, the job of the trade-union leader is becoming just as difficult as that of the politician. For he too is trapped between the demands of his union members and the pressure to turn him into an agent of Government policy in the name of a loudly-proclaimed national interest. For however vulnerable his membership are to that same national rhetoric, they are bound to find that the reality of Government policy involves a cut in their living standards and degree of job security. The ease with which trade-union leaders can weather this cross pressure turns, as the Government appears to realise full well, on the degree to which rank-and-file trade unionists can be persuaded to believe that inflation is their fault, when manifestly it is not. We should not be surprised that the Government is prepared to spend millions of pounds advertising its call for national restraint. The surprise, surely, is that its spending here is so little, and has come so late.

For it should be remembered that ideas play a crucial role in stabilising an unequal society. If, and only if, governments can persuade people on a large scale that what we are living through is not a crisis of 'capitalism' but one of 'democracy' will they be able to gain widespread support for their assertion that it is no longer legitimate to struggle against any Government policy which maintains or increases present inequalities. And in their attempt to win popular support, ministers have much going for them, including their generalised legitimacy, their access to the mass media, and the way in which the trade-unions' defensive actions are more visible than are the processes of capitalist exploitation which have really caused the crisis. All these will combine to persuade many people that a solution to inflation and uncompetitiveness is within our grasp at very little cost. Indeed it is for this reason that the spread of explanations of our current difficulties that fail to link them to the wider instabilities of capitalism are significant. For they help to persuade people that certain events and certain policies are inevitable, when in reality those events and policies are necessary only to maintain a particular, highly unequal system of private ownership and control. In the battle for public support, such arguments – and the parallel call by politicians for national restraint and trade-union moderation – gather force too, because they are related to that belief, so strong in British popular culture, that 'problems' necessarily have 'solutions' within the existing framework of government and property if only 'men of good faith' can act together 'responsibly'. It is therefore to be expected that Governments, industrialists, editors and even some trade-union leaders will continue to present our present difficulties in such terms and will bewail the absence of a national consensus without admitting how the consensus that they seek can only benefit privileged groups and injure the dispossessed so long as capitalist inequalities remain. For the task of governing Britain in the second half of the 1970s will be more or less easy for practising politicians precisely to the degree to which their view of things becomes generally shared, and trade unions and their members can be persuaded to accept cuts in their living standards and power. Politicians will strive endlessly to persuade people to accept cut-backs and unemployment without disturbing the existing distribution of wealth, income and power. But they will find that the pressures generated by capitalist instability and inequality will always militate against any permanent creation of such a general consensus against trade union action. Although Governments will call repeatedly for unity and co-operation, they will find that there is no easy solution to the tension between capital and labour in a world of international capitalism. The problems will not go away. On the contrary, as the crisis deepens, the problems of governing Britain will grow ever larger.

# NOTES

I would like to thank Joan Skidmore, Diane Elson, Dorothy Coates and David Skidmore for their help in the preparation of this chapter.

1 Roy Jenkins, *What Matters Now* (London: Fontana, 1972), p. 44.

2 J. H. Westergaard, 'Sociology: the myth of classlessness' in R. Blackburn, ed., *Ideology in Social Science* (London: Fontana, 1972), p. 156.

3 For a discussion of the character of the power structure in Britain, see R. Miliband, *The State in Capitalist Society* (London: Weidenfeld and Nicholson, 1969); also P. Stanworth and A. Giddens, eds., *Elites and Power in British Society* (Cambridge: Cambridge University Press, 1974); and J. Urry and J. Wakeford, eds., *Power in Britain* (London: Heinemann, 1973).

4 For views contrary to those found here, see R. Dahrendorf, *Class and Class Conflict in Industrial Society* (London: Routledge and Kegan Paul, 1959); A. Crosland, *The Future of Socialism* (London: Cape, 1956); C. Kerr, *et al. Industrialism and Industrial Man* (Harmondsworth: Penguin, 1973); or M. Weber, *The Protestant Ethic and the Spirit of Capitalism* (London: Allen and Unwin, 1965).

5 K. Marx, *Capital, Volume I* (London: Dent, 1972), p. 156.

6 K. Marx, *The Communist Manifesto* (1848) in *Marx-Engels, Selected Works* (London: Lawrence and Wishart, 1968), pp. 38 and 40.

7 A. Glyn and B. Sutcliffe, 'The collapse of U.K. profits', *New Left Review, 66* (March–April, 1971), p. 16.

8 M. Barratt Brown, *From Labourism to Socialism* (Nottingham: Spokesman Books, 1972), p. 39.

9 Glyn and Sutcliffe, 'Collapse of U.K. profits', p. 19.

10 Barratt Brown, *From Labourism to Socialism,* p. 193.

11 On this, see A. Glyn and B. Sutcliffe, *British Capitalism, Workers and the Profits Squeeze* (Harmondsworth: Penguin, 1972); and the National Institute for Economic and Social Research *Review*, No. 70, November, 1974, pp. 20–92.

12 For a fuller discussion of this, it is worth trying to obtain a copy of the Autumn 1973 *Bulletin of the Conference of Socialist Economists*, possibly from the Institute of Development Studies at the University of Sussex.

13 For a discussion of the relationship between trade unions and inflation, see D. Jackson, H. A. Turner and F. Wilkinson, *Do Trade Unions Cause Inflation?* (Cambridge: Cambridge University Press, 1975).

14 For details of this, see A. Flanders, *Management and Unions* (London: Faber, 1975); K. Hawkins, *Conflict and change : aspects of Industrial Relations* (London: Holt, Rinehart and Winston, 1972); and *Workplace Industrial Relations* (London: HMSO, 1968).

15 *Labour's Programme 1973* (London: Labour Party, 1973), p. 7.

16 David Coates, *The Labour Party and the Struggle for Socialism* (Cambridge: Cambridge University Press, 1975). That not everyone agrees with my analysis should be obvious from the range of opinions expressed in this collection of essays. See also the reviews of *The Labour Party and the Struggle for Socialism* by Anthony King (*New Society*, 20 February 1975) and John Mackintosh (*The Listener*, 6 March 1975).

# The disappearing consensus

Norman St John-Stevas

## Introduction

'Britain is becoming harder to govern.' Is this just another complaint from those who remember Queen Victoria's Empire? There is considerable evidence to suggest that it is not. The central reason why Britain is becoming harder to govern is the failure of government. In 1951, 1964, 1970 and 1974, the outgoing Governments were defeated Governments. They were defeated by the problems facing them and their own inability to surmount them. The Conservative Governments between 1951 and 1959, it is true, were a comparative success. At least they managed to win general elections in 1951, 1955 and 1959, but the trend ended in 1964. The new Labour Government of Harold Wilson found itself facing worsening economic problems, which have dogged Britain ever since. The Labour Government of 1964–1970 failed to solve our major economic problems. It left the country in a worse state than when it took over, notwithstanding its successful handling of the balance of payments problem. Standards of living rose, but very slowly. Ironically enough, the lasting achievements of the Labour Government were in the field of law reform rather than in the fields of social and economic policy.

The new Conservative Government of 1970 was left with worse economic troubles than Labour had inherited in 1964. It failed to solve them. The Industrial Relations Act soured relations with the trade unions, the energy crisis undermined the policy of economic expansion, the miners' strike challenged the rule of law, and the sovereignty of Parliament. Mr Heath then used the ultimate deterrent, dissolved Parliament and called a general election. The danger of a Prime Minister's using the final weapon is that if it is not successful he disarms not only himself but his successors. This is exactly what happened. The nation declined to give unequivocal backing to the Government – a dramatic shift in political power to the trade unions was the result, pointed up starkly by the defeat.

No Government in Britain can hope to succeed today without the goodwill of the unions. This was the consideration that dictated the terms of the 'social contract' in its first phase. It is equally true of its second counter-inflationary phase. Yet there is still no alternative source of direct political power. The armed forces, in contrast with those of France and Spain, have not played a direct part in British politics since the seventeenth century. The legitimacy of government is sustained in part by the lack of credible alternatives.

## A common sense of values essential to democracy

Any community will have certain moral ideas and ideals in common. Without some fundamental concepts held in this way, a society would disintegrate. This basic consensus constitutes the 'common possession' of society. As Newman said,

> a State is in its very idea a society, and a society is a collection of many individuals made one by their participation in some common possession, and to the extent of that common possession, held in common, constitutes the life, and the loss of it constitutes the dissolution, of a State.[1]

This common possession is reflected in the law and in the structure of Government. In Britain, as elsewhere in Western society, there is a connection between law and the moral sense of the community as real as the connection of law with a sanction. On certain issues the law may lag behind a little, on others it may be in advance, but broadly, it reflects the consensus. The prevailing morality produces the sort of body of law that would be expected.

59

This is not to suggest that there is unanimous agreement on all moral questions. We live in a pluralist society, where people adhere to many diverse creeds. In such a society, Government can only be Government by discussion. The continuous dialogue of all who wish to take part in it rests, however, on certain predetermined concepts. Without some basis of agreement, communication is not possible. Justice, truth, peace, order, reason and logic are still held in regard in our society, but support for them is weakening. Certain sections of society no longer accept these values as fundamental. The IRA, for example, has little time for peace and order. These anti-social forces are nothing new, but today they command more support.

The increasing difficulty of government in Britain is in part the result of moral and religious decline. It is in part the consequence of a crisis of confidence in government, and in the community. It is also a result of dramatic social change. All these things have made it more difficult to govern. There has been a definite decline in respect for Parliament, law and authority. The examples that come most easily to mind are the trade unions' defiance of the 1971 industrial relations legislation, the Clay Cross councillors' refusal to charge correct rents, and the Shrewsbury Two incident.

(a)  Decline in religious allegiance and belief

In the last thirty years, there has been a marked decline in the number of members of nearly all of the churches in Britain.[2] The established church, the Church of England, has suffered particularly badly. Certain rather obscure sects, some Christian, others Oriental in origin, have increased their memberships, but they remain on the fringe of society, and have little effect, even now, on mainstream Western thought and culture. The churches have suffered a decline in membership before, it is true. In the eighteenth century, the Church of England suffered a similar unpopularity, but the 'chapel' arose to fill the gap. People left one Christian church for another. There appears to be no similar revival in the separation of some new, impassioned, evangelical churchlet from the tired main body of the Church of England : 'Jesus freaks' are hardly to be compared with Wesley and his followers.

This decline in religious allegiance is almost certainly paralleled by a decline in actual religious belief. There are many people, it is true, who profess to be practising Christians while never setting foot in a church between baptism, marriage and death. But there are also many, for the first time in Britain, who have no religious beliefs whatsoever. It is doubtful whether the provision of the 1944 Education Act prescribing compulsory religious education in all schools would be passed today.

This situation contrasts with that on the continent of Europe. In most of these countries, religions, usually in the form of Roman Catholicism, has been more tenacious. Indeed, the Roman Catholic Church has been least hard-hit of all the major churches in this country by loss of members. Religion has retained its place in the forefront of public consciousness not only in a comparatively backward country like Spain, but also in advanced countries such as France and Italy. The Roman Catholic Church has retained her influence as a social, political and economic, as well as a religious, force in Europe. In this country, on the other hand, the Church of England has little social and political influence .

This has had three effects upon government in Britain. Firstly, the church has faded from the public eye in political matters. This is well illustrated by the history of the change in the abortion laws. The conflict was fought out by secular forces on both sides. No British church plays an active part in politics. In many ways this is a wise decision on their part, since foreign churches have from time to time burnt their fingers badly. Churches are, after all, selling a religious not a political programme. By identifying themselves with particular political attitudes and solutions they compromise their universal mission. However this has necessarily weakened the forces in politics that would normally expect to have the support of churches and of a religious sanction.

The second effect is a particular manifestation of the first. In several European countries, political parties have developed that draw upon religious support. West Germany and Italy have Christian Democratic parties. Belgium, Luxembourg and Switzerland have Christian Social parties. In the Netherlands, there are separate Calvinist, Protestant, Nonconformist and Catholic parties. Meanwhile, in Britain, no political party based upon a religious affiliation has developed. Even the old allegiances of Nonconformists to the Liberal party and of Anglicans to the Conservative party have been shown by Butler and Stokes to have largely fallen away, at least in conscious terms.[3]

The third effect of church decline on government has been in terms of psychology. It is difficult to assess whether this is a cause of the decline or an effect of it; probably it is both. With the decline of the churches, they have ceased to influence the public outlook as powerfully as once they did. Of course, this will have altered people's characters in many ways, arguably leading to lower moral standards. In particular, churches tend to promote a respect for authority. This is because their own dogma usually has respect for divine authority as the central theme. Though outwardly less hierarchical in structure, Nonconformist churches share with the others a fundamentally authoritarian outlook, at least as far as theology is concerned.

(b)   Weakened sense of community

The obvious way in which a weakened sense of community has revealed itself is in the weaknesses of the smaller communities into which society is divided. Manifestations of this weakened sense of community are easy to find : low turnout in elections, vandalism, the indifference of members of the public, even when they witness the commission of crimes. The decline in the sense of community has been accompanied by a growth in apathy. Its principal facet is apathy towards the fate of the nation. Patriotism has declined as a force and there is little agreement on what constitutes the public interest. The precise relationship between national apathy, unpatriotic tendencies and lack of agreed public interest is difficult to establish, but these three factors combine to make government more difficult by making the ground less certain under the government's feet. The impossibility of defining precisely an elusive phrase like 'the public interest' illustrates the discord presently surrounding it.

The second result is the growing vociferousness of minorities. The post-war period has seen a proliferation of pressure groups advocating every cause from nuclear disarmament to stopping a South African cricket tour. Some of these groups are prepared to use any means to attain their ends, though these may be against the national interest. It is this, rather than their existence itself, that makes government difficult. Fortunately, most restrict themselves to lawful pressure on the Government. It is an even greater temptation for a Government to give in to demands of powerful pressure groups than it is to submit to the tyranny of the majority. One standard by which to judge a Government's success would be the extent to which it mediates between the many factions in society to secure a balanced settlement, and the extent to which it protects the parts of society unable to protect themselves. Clearly, the more aggressive the pressure groups, the easier it becomes for the Government to sacrifice the public interest in return for peace and quiet.

(c) Decline in national confidence

The decline in national confidence has been the result of a receding empire and economic failure. It is natural that lack of success in the postwar world should leave the nation less than confident for the future. The mood of the nation is now one of pessimism. There have been many failures in foreign affairs since the war. If the United Nations were being established today, would Britain still be awarded a place in the Security Council? We have not only slipped from our place as a great power – an inevitable development as the peoples of the Commonwealth attained self-determination – but we have been demoralised by the better record of countries of similar size and status such as France and West Germany. This has been closely linked to the great post-war failure of British politics : the missing of the European bus.

In the immediate post-war years, the theme of Europe was reconstruction. In 1951 the European Coal and Steel Community was established in Paris, in order to create a situation in which, with basic materials under common control, war between the participating nations would be impossible. We did not participate in the ECSC. We also ignored the European Economic Community and Euratom, created in Rome in 1957. We then decided, having thrown away the chance to participate in European co-operation from the beginning, to apply for membership. In 1961, after we had organised a looser free trade area 'of our own', EFTA, Mr Harold Macmillan and Mr Edward Heath opened negotiations for entry. In 1963, the application was vetoed by France and Mr Wilson's application was vetoed again by France in 1967. Then on 3 January 1972, Mr Heath's second set of negotiations was successfully concluded, but the terms were not nearly as favourable as they would have been had we been founder members.

## (d) The revolution in expectations

Between the Black Death in 1348–49 and the last quarter of the nineteenth century, the standard of living of the mass of the population hardly altered. Rural society lived at little more than subsistence level. The consumer society is a creature of the twentieth century. Because living standards have generally risen for the last century, people expect their living standards to continue to rise. The question now is, 'Can ever higher living standards be delivered by Government?' The answer, as far as Britain is concerned, seems to be, 'Not for the time being'. The doubt in this connection has led to a further decline in respect for Government, and in people's willingness to accept its economic measures.

I have sought to show that a common set of values is essential to democracy and that this set of values is increasingly blurred in this country. The situation has been exacerbated by the decline in national confidence and the revolution in expectations. Formerly, national confidence and low expectations or, more recently, satisfied high expectations have distracted public attention from the erosion of values going on beneath the surface.

## The interdependence of society

### (a)  Interdependence as a fact of life

As the structure of society has become more complex, so the vast majority of citizens have become more dependent on each other for the necessities and luxuries of life. The total amount of trade is greater than ever before. Therefore, the total number of trading relationships is greater. Relatively few people today produce sufficient of the necessities to keep themselves alive. Most citizens today are engaged in manufacturing or service industries. This inevitably means we are more dependent on more people for more things than ever before. The scope for breakdown has increased and it is true that individual dependency relationships are more subject to breakdown today than in previous periods. The place of the Government, at the top of the pyramid, is in some ways more vulnerable than in the past. Not only is the Government dependent upon somebody for everything, but the Government is held generally responsible. The Government is called to account when things go wrong : it has to step in and pick up the pieces when some important dependency relationship fails.

The fact of interdependence has one important side-effect : to run an interdependent society at all efficiently requires a high degree of organisation. This is not always compatible with democracy. Of course, in order to live in any type of society, the citizens must surrender some of their freedoms, but in the complex conditions of modern society more freedoms have to be surrendered than in earlier times. An army of bureaucrats is now necessary to enforce equally numerous regulations covering all facets of life. Most of this corpus was not necessary until recently. While the necessity of rules is recognised, it is also true that each new rule removes a freedom of some sort.

## (b) Experts

A phenomenon of the second half of the twentieth century is dependence on experts. Advanced technology requires advanced knowledge, and this means more experts. Experts are needed for a whole range of technical jobs; people have to rely on experts to service their machines where once there were no machines, and, therefore, no experts. More relevant still to the difficulty of Government is the special position experts occupy. Society is now so advanced that the Government requires expert advice at every turn. Because of the multiplication of categories of skills, as the world becomes more complex, it has become difficult to take a balanced, general and informed view. There is a lack of unity in Government direction owing to the difficulty of taking an overall but still expert view. Experts themselves are naturally insensitive to political factors; they have been trained to be knowledgeable only in their particular field. The experts who are more and more powerful in a technological society lack political responsibility. The remedy for this must lie in a broader approach in education to preserve some flexibility, and the training of leaders able to make informed decisions, taking into account political and social as well as technical considerations with some competence. Perhaps emphasis ought now to be placed on the production of polymaths rather than specialists : on comprehensive education in the true sense of the phrase. We have to produce leaders who are experts in general knowledge – in the sense of Leonardo and Mill.

*Defects in government machinery*

(a) Generation of policy

The attitude of the general public to Government policy tends to be suspicious and sullen. The people do not necessarily reject Government advice, but acceptance is grudging. A Government's policy may very well be condemned merely because it is Government policy, and without much rational consideration of the policy itself. This situation has come about partly because of the disintegration of the hierarchical structure of society. Unfortunately, this disintegration has exposed a further flaw in our political system's democratic character. People naturally resent being told what to do, even though the orders themselves may be sensible and though they are given by an elected Government. The Government is elected democratically, but Government policy is not generated in a democratic way.

Policy decisions are made by the executive arm of the Government. It reaches those decisions, partly by bowing to the opinion of its own political party, partly because it believes those decisions to be necessary, having taken the advice of the appropriate civil servants. General direction is given by the personal preferences of its members, according to their relative importance. The Government's decisions are subject to minor amendment in Parliament, and Government spokesmen present the decisions, in an effort to persuade the public that they are in their interest.

What is missing in this is a sufficient element of public participation. Government decisions are a consequence not of pressure from below, in the sense of a response to general public feeling, but of the desire to plot a future course defined by the executive and made acceptable to the man in the street through propaganda and advertisement.

One example of the lack of influence of public opinion on policy decisions in Britain has been the obsession of successive Labour Governments with unnecessary, undesirable and costly nationalisation. It would be ridiculous to suggest that this policy has general public support. The stubbornness of an executive, even when public opinion is clearly and vocally against a policy, is also well illustrated by the years of agitation it took to persuade the executive in the United States that American troops should be withdrawn from Vietnam. Governments could show themselves more ready to bow to public opinion where this is unequivocal in its opposition to a particular line of policy.

(b)  Changes in the distribution of economic power

The most obvious, and probably the most important, change in the distribution of economic power in recent years has been the increasing power of the trade unions. Strikes over the past decade by miners, dockers, power workers and other key workers have illustrated the dependence of society upon them. These strikes culminated in the miners' strike of 1974. The Heath Government's confrontation with them finally exposed the weakness of Government faced with militant trade unions. Thus, a process already taking place was accelerated, in much the same way as the Suez incident highlighted and accelerated the decline of the British Empire. When Mr Heath used the ultimate weapon of the general election, he failed to secure the backing of the people.

The other important new power concentration consists of the multinational companies. These companies are sometimes larger in terms of their sales than many small countries' gross national products. The multinationals clearly pose a threat to such small countries, and a great deal has been made of the depredations of International Telephones and Telecommunications, in Chile for example. Yet larger countries also have problems with multinationals.

The root of the trouble is that, while the subsidiary of the multinational operating in Britain does its best to comply with the wishes of the Government, in the last resort, its loyalty is not to the Government but to some foreign parent company.

On the whole, British Governments have managed this problem well, though this is not to say that the problem does not exist, or that multinationals will not continue to raise problems about national independence in the future. In the motor industry, for example, in spite of threats from time to time of withdrawal, Chrysler, General Motors and Ford have maintained their plants in Britain. Some multinationals, such as Rio Tinto Zinc and Dunlop, are British-controlled. A new factor that should strengthen the position of the Government is our membership of the European Communities. As European co-operation develops, European policy towards multinationals will become easier to evolve. This is a field in which rapid development of community policy is essential if respect for government is to be maintained.

## (c) Constitution and representation

The constitutional machinery of government in Britain is fundamentally the same as it was in the eighteenth century. It is no wonder that it is beginning to creak under the strain of changed social and political conditions; indeed it is remarkable that the system has held up for so long. The British parliamentary system was exported to most Commonwealth countries when they attained their independence. In many of them it has not withstood the many pressures in a young country, and has been swept away in favour of military or totalitarian rule. Britain has been slow to develop constitutionally, despite the lack of a written constitution, or perhaps because of it. The system that has stood up in Britain, buttressed by centuries of tradition, has fallen in the Commonwealth without that buttress, and is now under challenge in the mother country itself.

A threatening development has been the progressive isolation of the executive arm of government. While the theoretical and constitutional government was in 1775 and still is in 1975 the Queen in Parliament, the effective centre of Government has been reduced in size. First, the monarchy ceased to play any significant role in government and power was exercised by Parliament alone. In 1911, the House of Lords was shorn of most of its effective say in government. The power of the Cabinet has declined, while that of the Prime Minister and the civil service has increased.[4] While various parts of the original system of government have been stripped of power, no alternative donees have been found for the power.

There are many ways in which this capacity freed by the concentration of power might be used constructively, though the present Government does not appear particularly well-disposed towards any of them. The first and most widely supported is devolution, both in the sense of the hiving off of functions and of devolution proper. The important effect that this could have on the power of the House of Commons is that, by delegating the more trivial legislation and so on to secondary bodies, the House of Commons would have much more time to scrutinise the really crucial work of government.

The second major reform possible is a change in the Upper House. While the valuable work done by the House of Lords is not to be despised, it lacks authority. The time is ripe for another attempt to create a Second Chamber with a sufficiently rational basis to command public support and to justify the conferring on it of increased powers. One idea worth considering is that put forward by Sir Winston Churchill in 1930, of a third chamber. This 'House of Industry' would deal with the problems posed by the trade unions and others, advising Parliament and preparing solutions to social and economic problems by bringing together unions, employers and Government.

There are in addition other minor reforms that could be

considered : a development of the Commons committee system, proportional representation, a geographically based second chamber, to name but a few. What is certain is the desirability of some reform of our constitution, to reflect the changed distribution of economic power in the nation.

## (d)  Remoteness of government

Contemporary man is coming to think that perhaps small is beautiful after all. The British government machine has many faults, but the most outstanding is its remoteness. The Government is increasingly thought of by the public as a body both cold and distant : 'The Government'. This remoteness is not only psychological, there is a real physical remoteness. Though Britain is a relatively small country, people on the fringe of Scotland can be a day's travel from London. If such people have a grievance, it is physically extremely difficult for them to take it up in person with representatives of government.

Two developments that have made matters worse in this respect have been the 1974 local government reorganisation and the development of super-ministries. The 1974 local government reform increased the size of the old local government units, thus removing one defect of the old system, but creating others. The super ministries have come about by the amalgamation of two or more old ministries. Thus we have the Department of the Environment where, before, were the Ministry of Public Buildings and Works, the Ministry of Housing and Local Government, the Ministry of Land and Natural Resources and the Ministry of Transport. The Department of Trade and Industry, now broken up, was composed in the same way, and the Foreign Office has swallowed up the Colonial Office and Commonwealth Relations Office. The real failure of both the super ministries and the enlarged counties has been their failure to inspire confidence.

Government must now respond to public wishes and devise policies to combat this remoteness. Devolution is an urgent need, not only to oil the wheels of government and to present a more human aspect, but, above all, to recreate confidence in the governmental process. Regional government might well provide a partial solution to this problem provided that more local institutions were retained or created which citizens would be familiar with and to which there would be easy access. The need is particularly acute in Scotland and Wales where government from London is resented as remote and ill-informed. There is no inconsistency between centralising certain functions of government and devolving others : both processes can occur at the same time.

Britain has become harder to govern in the second part of the twentieth century because of the pace of social and moral change for which our previous history provides no precedent. The consensus evolved over the centuries on what constitutes 'the good life' is in danger of dissolution into a welter of competing philosophies and viewpoints. Cynicism has replaced conviction. At the very time that the 'common possession' of society has been fragmented, interdependence has grown. The interior sanctions provided by an agreed moral and social outlook are disappearing at the very moment when they are most needed. History tends to be cyclical so that it may well be that this process will be reversed in the future, but there is no doubt that the 1970s have seen the emergence of a more general challenge to the legitimacy and effectiveness of government than has been seen before in this century. The violence at the opening of the century and the passions aroused then by social and industrial unrest were focused on particular issues and were susceptible of solution. What distinguishes the present decade is that the criticism and hostility towards government is of a more general character and is compounded by a cynicism on the part of many towards political institutions and those who take part in them.

# NOTES

1   J. H. Newman, *Historical Sketches* (London: B. M. Pickering, 1872–73), vol. 1, p. 161.

2   In the Church of England, for example, the numbers of Christmas and Easter parish communions fell from 2,074,000 and 2,339,000 in 1960 to 1,689,000 and 1,814,000 in 1970. Confirmations fell in the same period from 32.4 to 19.7 per thousand of the population of the appropriate age. The Roman Catholic Church has also recently reported a startling reduction in the number of converts.

3   David Butler and Donald Stokes, *Political Change in Britain: Forces Shaping Electoral Choice* (London: Macmillan, 1969), pp. 159–71.

4   This is not to accept the exaggerations of the late Mr R. H. S. Crossman. For a full discussion of the issues raised, see my edition of *The Works of Walter Bagehot*, volume V (London: The Economist, 1974), pp. 132–45.

# The declining respect for the law

John P. Mackintosh

The evening before the writing of this chapter was started, the author attended a meeting in the village of Earlston in the Scottish borders. Three hundred people were present to protest at a 246 per cent increase in the local rates. Towards the end of the meeting, in what is a deeply traditional and conservative rural area, a well-dressed man arose to move that all those present should refuse to pay rates till certain points had been met. The motion was later withdrawn but that it was moved at all in such a community was amazing.

Yet MPs of all parties find themselves going from one meeting to another where forceful actions or breaches of the law are proposed. In recent months, the author has been asked to support the Scottish school teachers' strike, the blockade of ports by inshore fishermen and several suggested rate and rent strikes. Nor are MPs themselves immune from making such calls. Mr Russell Johnston, the MP for Inverness, has urged the withholding of taxes till proportional representation is conceded. A majority of the Parliamentary Labour Party voted in their party meeting and then in the House of Commons for the retrospective withdrawal of the proper legal disqualification imposed on the councillors at Clay Cross who had refused to implement the Housing Finance Act of 1972, while other Labour MPs wanted to overturn the court's decision in the case of two men found guilty of intimidation while picketing a building site in Shrewsbury.

In addition to demands by local groups and similar suggestions by MPs, reputable pressure groups contemplate or carry through actions intended to break a law or defy the Government. Two successive Governments, one Labour, the other Conservative, attempted to alter the law dealing with industrial relations and to impose a statutory incomes policy, and in each case the policies had to be abandoned because of the opposition of powerful pressure groups. Over industrial relations, the unions were able to swing round enough Labour MPs and then the Labour Cabinet to stop the introduction of a bill in 1969 based on the White Paper, *In Place of Strife*. The Conservatives were able to carry their bill into law but it was boycotted by the TUC and disobeyed by several unions. It largely ceased to be implemented while it was on the statute book and was finally repealed by the incoming Labour Government.

But Governments themselves act in a way outside the law and, in so doing, indicate their attitude towards laws and the process of law-making. In a Granada television programme on 'The State of the Nation', Sir William Armstrong, then still head of the civil service, said that when he had been a young official and a minister proposed certain actions, these were abandoned directly the official said, in effect, 'But, minister, you have no such powers.'[1] Now it is common for the minister (in whatever party) to say, 'Very well, we will introduce the appropriate legislation and meanwhile I will announce my intention to enforce these proposals. The bill will give the Government retrospective authority.' At the time of writing, there is a letter in *The Times* pointing out that the Government is advertising posts in a new Welsh Land Authority which is proposed under legislation presently passing through the Commons. Actions are being taken to implement a law which cannot receive the royal assent for several months.

The question is why both Government and the governed, Members of Parliament and electors, pressure groups and civil servants, have come to take this view of the law, to remove it from the rather special reverence it had a century ago so that at times they contemplate breaking the law without any sense that this is a dangerous matter and is, in a strict sense, criminal activity.

## Governmental failures

If the question is put to ordinary members of the public, 'Why are you proposing to break the law?', the answer usually comes in two forms. The first is to explain the frustrations or governmental failures that have led to the situation. Fishermen explain soaring costs, sagging prices, voice their fears about a 'sell out in Brussels' or their alarms about foreign fishing fleets operating within the present fishing limits and their lack of confidence in the government's understanding of their problems. When trade unionists are asked why they are prepared to strike against an incomes policy that has been enacted by Parliament, they point to prices, to rents, to their general sense that their economic expectations have not been met. Their sense is of Governments that do not know or care about their case. Clearly this is not an explanation given by MPs, pressure group leaders or civil servants when they ignore, belittle or defy the law, so it is by no means a complete or adequate explanation. Nevertheless, it does seem to be true that, if post-war British Governments had been markedly more successful, if the British standard of living had shot up and if we were as much richer than the Germans and the French as we were in the period just after the war, and therefore more successful and self-confident, then there would be, if not a greater willingness to obey laws, at least far fewer occasions when there was any temptation to break them.

## The efficacy of direct action

The second response, perhaps even more common than the first, but one which usually follows on the complaints about governmental policies and failures, is the observation that this is the only way to achieve anything. People at once say, 'It worked for the miners. Why not for us?' When striking school teachers were asked what example they thought they were giving to their pupils, the reply was always in terms of

76

'this is the only way to make the Government listen' or 'if you go according to the rules, you get nowhere'.

Several thoughts occur at once. The first is that this goes deeper as an explanation than mere complaints about governmental failures. After all, Governments failed to achieve their objectives long before recent decades and yet were able to secure obedience. Now this response indicates a lack of confidence in the democratic procedures for obtaining redress of grievances or changes in policy. Also, the response pinpoints a failure of democratic machinery, as many would regard this reply as reasonable in certain kinds of dictatorships. If citizens in a dictatorship said they had to demonstrate or riot or break laws, there would be little if any readiness to question the propriety of such action; the only issue would be whether this was a safe or sensible way to behave. But the traditional view in Western democracies is that because established procedures exist for pressing a point of view, for seeking to change policies, and because most voters have indicated their acceptance of these procedures by taking part in elections, it is wrong to go outside or defy the system. Just because there is a method of compromising between the demands of individuals and of majority and minority groups, it is assumed that, when a demand is not met, this is because it has not met with sufficient favour or won sufficient support to become the established policy of the whole community. Again, to break the rules to enforce conduct or views that have not been accepted in this way seems to be challenging the framework of the society; it seems to be insisting on the rule of force rather than the rule of law and, if every person or group acted in this way, the society in its existing form would collapse.

When points of this kind are put to potential law-breakers, they elicit a variety of responses. (These are practical observations as the author has on four occasions attended protest meetings where such actions have been proposed and has opposed such suggestions.) The first response is the one already mentioned. It is a repetition of 'if it is all right for others, why not for us?' This only takes us back to square one.

A second response, which is often heard, is really a criticism of the system of communications. This is the assertion that direct action of some kind is the only way of bringing the issue to the attention of the decision-makers. The assumption is that if the representative or democratic system was working properly, then the policy being advocated would have been adopted. A further assumption is that, if the system could be seen to be working well and if the objectors' view was definitely and properly considered and rejected, then there would be no desire at that stage to go on and enforce the rejected view or policy by direct action. This is part of the case that the only way to get results is to press for them by means of disruption or law-breaking on the ground that the legislators or governors are too busy or ill-informed or insensitive to act on their own but in the belief that, when the matter is brought to their attention, they will accept the justice of the case.

Only a few go on and say that they would continue by direct action even if it was clear that, after full and proper consideration, their wishes were not those of the majority. But such groups do exist. These are the most consciously political elements. The extreme examples are the IRA, the Angry Brigade or the committed revolutionary groups who would persist whatever the reactions of the rest of the society. But it is interesting that these sections are a highly ideological minority. The vast bulk of those willing to break the law are deeply reluctant to accept that they are acting against the interests of the majority and indeed in a manner which, if universalised, would destroy the rule of law and civilised democratic society as it is known in the Western world.

Two further points are worth noting at a purely practical level. The first is that there is some validity in the claim that conduct of this kind does produce results. The wages of those groups who have challenged successive pay policies have improved more than those of docile groups who have accepted Government policy. The individuals who ruined the test match cricket pitch in order to draw attention to what they believed was the wrongful conviction of a Mr George Davis obtained an immediate Home Office inquiry into the case. Whatever the final outcome, the fishermen never had such concern shown about their problems as was forthcoming when the blockade of the ports was undertaken.

The second practical point is the weakness of the Governments concerned. They have shown an extreme lack of self-confidence in response to such pressure. They have half conceded the disruptors' argument by paying excessive attention to the pressure. This stretches from the view prevalent in large sections of both the Labour and Conservative parties not that an incomes policy is undesirable but that 'it will not work'. By this, what is meant is that, when challenged, Governments either cannot or will not rally the public, pass emergency laws or call out the troops, and in the end will cave in. Perhaps what underlies this belief is the fear, especially after Mr Heath took on the miners in February 1974 and lost, that the public will not back up the Government. However, this cannot be demonstrated, as the public might back up a vigorous, confident Government that knew what it wanted and showed that it was not going to be pushed around. But successive British Governments have only shown their weakness and, in this sense, they have half endorsed the objectors' case that Governments only respond to threats or violence and that, moreover, once these occur, the policies that have been pressed in this way are not only accepted but are accepted in a manner which shows that they are not unwelcome to the majority of the community. From this, it follows that certain questions must be asked. Is the democratic machinery sluggish and slow? Does it fail to bring genuine popular demands to the fore? Is there something wrong with the representative system as it is now practised in Britain and other Western countries?

The weakness of the House of Commons, in the sense that people no longer feel that passage of a measure by the House is an adequate indication of public approval, is endemic. It arises in many instances where there is no question of any consequential disobedience by the public. Perhaps the best example is the British decision to join the European Economic Community. In October 1971 the question of membership was put to the House. The Labour whips were employed to obtain a 'No' vote but sixty-nine Labour MPs defied the whip and voted 'Yes' while twenty more abstained. As a result of this assertion of the views of the House of Commons, despite all attempts at party dictation, there was a majority of 112 for British membership. Yet the Conservative Prime Minister, Mr Edward Heath, felt he had to say that he would not consider British membership was assured and final unless it was supported by 'the full-hearted consent of the British people'. Though he went on in the same sentence to say 'as expressed in Parliament', it was clear that in some sense neither he nor the public regarded the 112 majority as sufficient in itself. Perhaps it would have been enough had the opinion polls shown a favourable majority among the public at large. Perhaps it would have been enough had the Labour party as well as the Conservative party been clearly in favour of British membership. But the key point is that lacking a majority in the polls, lacking all-party support, a simple unwhipped (or whip-defying) majority of 112 was not enough to settle the question.

Later, in 1975, the House of Commons endorsed the principle of British membership by a majority of 226, but again this was not enough. When the people, on the other hand, gave a 68 per cent to 32 per cent vote in favour of membership in the referendum, this was conclusive. The argument in principle was settled. The question that arises is, what has happened to the House of Commons that its decisions no longer have the force of the referendum, that a clear majority in the House no longer carries adequate weight? Obviously this has something to do with the public's feeling either that the democratic process is slow, unresponsive to public opinion or simply out of touch, or that the process does not reflect the voters' real views.

In trying to explain the situation, it may be best to look back at the classic period of British representative democracy when there was a much more positive feeling that laws passed by Parliament had received popular assent, that such laws were legitimate and should be obeyed. These laws were clearly set apart from the ordinary conventions of good behaviour, which could be ignored, abandoned or violated if this seemed to be in the interest of an individual or of an organized and determined group in the community.

How then is it possible to explain the efficacy and supremacy of law in the heyday of the nineteenth-century parliamentary system in Britain? If we look at the speeches of politicians and the standard texts from Bagehot to Lowell, certain points emerge. The main one is that the consent-giving model was clear and comprehensible and was positively enforced. The model that was explained to the public went as follows. Electors choose an MP in each constituency. These MPs meet and choose a Prime Minister who, with the rest of the Cabinet, presents the Government's policies and measures to the House of Commons. These same MPs are able to, and do, reject or amend laws and are also able, by a more definite combination on what is clearly an issue of confidence, to get rid of the Government. But while the administration remains acceptable, most of its measures will be passed.

Once a law was passed, a minister responsible to the House of Commons and under its day-by-day supervision had the task of carrying out the law. His civil servants executed his commands. They did not make policy or advise on its content; they carried out the minister's instructions. As a result, the public were governed by laws made by ministers whom they had chosen, albeit indirectly. An interesting confirmatory point is that it was considered wrong for pressure groups to see civil servants. Pressure groups could only communicate with departmental officials in writing. If such groups wanted to exercise influence, they could only do so through the legitimate centre of political decision-making, the House of Commons, by dealing directly with ministers and MPs. This is why the original executive of the TUC, founded in 1868, was called 'the Parliamentary Committee', because its chief task was to lobby MPs. Other groups such as the East and West India trading interests, the Anti-Corn Law League, the railway company directors and even the nonconformist churches, either sought to elect a certain number of their members to Parliament or sought to keep the backing of a body of interested and sympathetic MPs.

So the 'consent model' was relatively simple and easily understood by the public. Everything was channelled through Parliament. All those wanting to influence policy worked on MPs. These representatives were relatively free from party control (though close to their constituents) and they voted as they thought proper. In consequence, the measures passed after long, probing debates, with amendments moved and accepted, were regarded as proper laws bearing the consent of the people. These were special commandments which it was assumed the public would accept as something requiring obedience.

What has happened to this concept? The basic change has been an elaboration of political and administrative life which has confused the old 'consent model' by introducing new forms of consent, of public endorsement of policies, so that it is no longer clear when a bill or act is fully legitimate. But the outcome is certainly to suggest that endorsement by a majority in the House of Commons is not any longer enough of itself.

The new forms of consent intrude at different points in the process of decision-making. One form is the assertion that policies or laws are not legitimate unless they have been included in the victorious party's election manifesto and have therefore received some kind of endorsement by the electorate. It was said again and again that the House of Commons' vote in favour of British membership of the EEC in 1971 was not sufficient because the then Conservative Government had stated in its previous election manifesto, 'Our commitment is to negotiate . . . nothing more; nothing less.' According to this view, Governments can act to meet new and developing situations but may not carry out overall policies or enact important items of legislation unless these have been endorsed by the voters. Hence Mr Wilson's effort to demonstrate that the £6 limit in wage increases in 1975–76 was not a statutory incomes policy in the terms in which such a policy had been repudiated in this party's most recent election manifesto.

The peculiar feature of this new form of consent is that, while most Governments in Britain are elected on 40 to 45 per cent of the popular vote, the manifesto policies are often the work of small groups in the party or (in the case of Labour) of the National Executive Committee, and passage by the Annual Party Conference does not alter this fact. But the idea or force behind the effort to introduce some kind of popular mandate into British politics is fairly clear. The idea is that parties and MPs cannot be left to devise or adapt policies based on their general philosophies as new situations arise. Policies are not legitimate unless they have been put to and endorsed by the electorate. It is clearly impossible for all the things a Government may want to do in the last two years of a parliament to have been foreseen in the run up to a general election years earlier. Also, many Governments are forced to abandon policies on which they fought the last election (making U-turns as it is colloquially described). But all such new or reversed policies have the shadow cast over them that they are not fully legitimate. If there is a desire to repudiate these policies among the public or to resist the laws in which they are embodied, then the argument will be used that the Government has no mandate to act in this way or to call for obedience. The problem is not that this is a new and clear requirement for laws if they are to be legitimate, in addition to passage by the House of Commons (and the Lords). The difficulty is that this is a source of legitimacy which is only half accepted, sometimes used and sometimes disregarded, so that its existence leads to an element of confusion.

This confusion over the mandate leads to a similar confusion over the position of MPs and how they should behave. Most Members of Parliament are used to being told that no one can have any respect for their judgement so long as they are mere lobby-fodder, being marshalled by the party whips to vote for measures which, though listed in the party manifesto, they have not considered and approved of themselves. But perhaps the very same person on the same occasion, given a different context, can ask the MP, 'Why did you vote for X when this is not part of the party's policy? We did not send you to Parliament to act in an élitist, eighteenth-century manner exercising your own judgement. We sent you there to put through Labour policies.' The lack of clarity (very marked compared with the late Victorian period) over the value and meaning of representative democracy tends to mean that MPs and Parliament lose or are blamed whatever they do. If ever there was an occasion when Parliament broke ranks and voted according to Members' views of the country's interest, it was in the 1971 vote of principle in favour of British membership of the EEC. Yet that this was so gave this 'free' act no greater validity than all the normal whipped votes where each MP votes his party ticket. And many MPs were attacked in their constituencies for making up their own minds (though only one, Mr Dick Taverne, was actually refused renomination because of this). But had all those Labour MPs who had voted for the application to join the EEC in 1967 and who were open and avowed Europeans changed their minds or at least their conduct and obeyed the party whip, there would have been a torrent of criticism of the two-faced invertebrates, the weak-kneed time-servers who were destroying the reputation of a once free and great Parliament.

Besides the weakening of Parliament's authority caused by this confusion over whether consent comes directly from the public in the form of a mandate for a party programme or whether it comes from the judgement exercised by those elected to represent the people, there is a further intrusion into the old simple consent model which adds further confusion and weakness. This is the role of the major pressure groups. Because Government does so much more and intervenes so much more than it did in the last century, the old doctrine that pressure groups can only reach the administration through MPs or ministers has long been abandoned. Part of the same process has been the end of the notion that civil servants merely execute policies decided on by ministers and authorised by Parliament. It is now accepted that officials do not merely advise on policy but, in many areas, actually make policy. As a result, pressure groups seek and gain direct access to Whitehall departments. This right to access by recognised bargaining groups is now an established convention of governmental practice (what passes in this country for a constitution). Groups are admitted to this status on the understanding that they represent a sizeable proportion of their clientele and that they will preserve the confidentiality of all discussions with officials. In return, they receive the right to consultation before and during the framing of policies and of legislation. (There is a curious hangover from the old days when Parliament was supposed to frame or be the first to see proposed legislation. The civil servants will not show the pressure groups' members the draft clauses of a bill but they will discuss and explain and negotiate the content of the clauses.)

Thus pressure groups play an established part in the legislative process, and a more important part than is played by MPs in Parliament, as the former take part in the bargaining that produces the legislation while the two Houses of Parliament are called in only when the work is complete and the legislature is presented with the finished article. This is reinforced by the fact that for practical purposes no amendments can be carried against the Government while bills are passing through the House (Professor Griffith has isolated the handful of cases where this has happened during three parliamentary sessions in his *Parliamentary Scrutiny of Government Bills*).[2]

The results of this practice are far-reaching. First, the fact that there is now a conventional right to this kind of consultation means that, if the right is withheld or if relations between the pressure group and the Government break down or are very strained, then it may be claimed that the resulting legislation lacks consent, that it is not fully legitimate and even that it need not be obeyed. For instance, the National Farmers' Union, prior to British membership of the European Community, used to have an annual series of private meetings with the Ministry of Agriculture and the Treasury at which the Annual Determination of Prices was made. If the negotiation was acceptable to the NFU, it announced that it was an 'agreed' review. But in some years, when the NFU felt it had lost too much, it announced that it had refused to accept the review. (It used to be said that the Government kept some £2 million in reserve in order, it was hoped, to throw in this sum at the end in concessions to obtain the NFUs consent.)

But what did it mean if the review was declared to be unacceptable? Were farmers to refuse to co-operate with the Government? Clearly in some sense, doubt was cast on the legitimacy of the outcome. When the Conservatives came to power in 1970, they had already done most of the work on their Industrial Relations Bill. They wanted to enact it quickly and they knew that the TUC would not accept it so they did not go through the customary negotiations with the unions. In consequence, the TUC said that they had no obligation to accept or obey the measure; they called on their members to boycott the court set up by the bill and refused to register their organisations under the terms of the bill. Eventually, large sections of the act were not operated and the incoming Labour Government repealed it at once.

So what has happened is that there has been introduced into the old, simple system of parliamentary consent-giving a further source of consent, the approval of the pressure groups. Not only does this raise the consequential issue of whether laws or policies are fully valid if this consent is refused, but it has two further effects. One is to raise the question in the public's mind of whether they are better represented through their pressure group or through their Member of Parliament. Secondly, the status and efficacy of MPs and of Parliament is further reduced. Many people organise themselves into groups in the belief that only in this way can they have an effective voice in matters concerning them. This is why there has been a flood of members to join an organisation for the self-employed. Facing extra insurance payments and taxes, the conclusion of the self-employed was not to see their MP or join a political party but to form a union. When a group of those organised in some body are contemplating direct action and are appealed to on the grounds that Britain is a democracy and that there is no need for them to go outside the normal procedures, their usual reply is that these procedures are too slow and achieve little or nothing. What is also significant is that those who vote against such direct action, if they are in a minority, usually decide that to refuse to go along with the majority would be to weaken the organised group and thus prevent it from working effectively for its members. Loyalty to the pressure group thus comes before loyalty to democratic procedures and institutions.

All this downgrades Parliament and gives people some justification when they contemplate refusing to obey a law passed by Parliament. It is evident that the leaders of industry, the professions and the unions prefer to work in their various organisations and to remain outside Parliament because they have more influence on decision-making and even on legislation in this way. Through the right to prior consultation they can play a larger and more effective part than the trade unionists or industrialists or professional men who get themselves elected to Parliament.

The most extreme instance of these tendencies has been over incomes policy. Mr George Brown, seeking his 'Declaration of Intent' with the unions, naturally indulged in direct negotiations. When Mr Heath turned to an incomes policy, he held a long-drawn out series of tripartite meetings with the CBI and TUC, while Parliament stood in the wings ready to enact whatever was agreed upon at these negotiations. Similarly, Mr Wilson, when he turned to such a policy in 1975, worked assiduously not only to acquire trade-union support for it but to have the initiative for the policy that he was going to adopt come from a union leader, Mr Jack Jones. It was not a question of whether, with a majority of one, he could put the legislation through the House. The question was whether he could get the support of both sides of industry. If this was forthcoming and particularly if the National Union of Mineworkers agreed, then not only would it be possible to enforce the policy but he could be sure of passing the necessary measures, since if the unions agreed the left wing of the Labour party would offer only token opposition in Parliament.

So, for all these reasons, it is not surprising if the public do not consider mere passage by a majority in the Commons sufficient to confer a special moral authority on laws. They want to know whether their pressure groups have been consulted and have agreed, whether the proposal was in the party manifesto and whether the measure has evident public support. The old, straightforward parliamentary system of democracy has been added to and been confused by other concepts of legitimacy and other methods of obtaining and demonstrating support, the total result of which is to take away the automatic reverence for the process of law and to make people ask, 'Why should I?', 'What is in this for me?', 'How am I affected?', and 'Can I see the point of this regulation?'.

## The nature of modern law

When these questions are asked, the answer is less clear than it used to be when laws dealt largely with inter-personal behaviour and usually merely reinforced moral precepts. It is clearly anti-social to break laws against stealing and this can be extended to cover fraud, sending over-loaded unseaworthy ships to sea or allowing women and children to work in the kind of conditions that existed in nineteenth-century coal mines. Laws like these, moreover, could be easily enforced. A breach of the law was obvious and elementary policing could detect and apprehend offenders. By the same token, most people knew when they were breaking such laws. At that time, large areas of social and economic activity were thought to be outside the scope of the law. It was thought that attempts to regulate the economy, the level of employment, welfare matters and the wages of adult male workers were not only wrong but impossible.

In the period since the 1930s, this concept of an area of life where state action and legal intervention are improper and fruitless has disappeared. The state and therefore the various legislating bodies have extended the state's competence over the economy, particular industries, the welfare system and many aspects of social relations (such as race relations). Now, in contrast to the position a hundred years ago, there is almost no area of life where politicians will reply to a 'What are you going to do about it?' question by saying, 'This lies quite outside the realm of state action.' This huge extension of the field actually or potentially open to legal intervention carries with it a number of serious problems.

First, it is possible to have laws making illegal actions performed by a group that are not only legal but even praiseworthy when done by a solitary individual. For instance, there is nothing wrong in a worker refusing to accept a job if he considers the pay is too low and there may even be a moral obligation on him to press for more money if the lower rate of pay proposed imposes undue hardships on his family. But there can be a law saying that, if all miners collectively refuse to work unless they get a pay rise in excess of a certain norm, this is an offence. So an activity that is normally acceptable and even admirable and whose alleged anti-social repercussions are by no means obvious can be transformed into an illegal activity. Another aspect of such laws is the apparent unfairness of any cut-off point. Thus a £6 per week maximum rise is enforced as from the 31 July 1975 but local government officials who obtained a 22 per cent increase a week before received their money, which was often well in excess of the £6 limit. In the 1967–69 incomes policy, the axe fell between a pay rise for English building workers and the consequent and normally automatic increase for their Scottish counterparts.

There are several other ways in which such laws can be unclear, which certainly makes it harder to maintain that law-breaking is an especially anti-social act. For instance, it is not always clear when laws of this kind have been broken. The 1975 incomes legislation allows employers to bargain with their workers and concede pay demands. Once conceded, the Department of Employment will examine them and say whether the total mix of bonuses, shift money, shorter hours, holiday pay and whatever else is involved does not exceed the £6 limit. So in marginal cases, it will be hard to know whether an offence is being committed. The law will only be broken when the minister issues a certificate to this effect. Also, it may be evident when moral laws are broken that the repetition of such acts could undermine a society. But many modern laws which affect the public are based on policy and reasonable people may disagree with the policy. To look again at incomes legislation, each set of laws on this subject has been passed to a chorus of comment that all such legislation is unworkable, undesirable and unlikely to do anything to combat inflation. Finally, there is the uncertainty created by the sheer volume of law – local by-laws, statutory instruments, British laws and now also the legislation of the European Community.

Putting together the weakness of Parliament, its lack of capacity to legitimise laws and the uncertainty, complexity and policy-embodying nature of much modern law, it is easier to see why powerful sections of the community, who may be affected and who may have been omitted from prior consultations (or whose objections may have been brushed aside), may contemplate ignoring, boycotting or disobeying certain laws. However, the assumption of much of this chapter has been that, if people did see the point of a law, if it did have clear majority support and if it had gone through all the modern phases and stages of obtaining legitimacy, then people would be willing to obey it. This is probably the case for the bulk of the community. But it is worth noting that there are small groups of people prepared to disobey laws despite all these conditions. They would be prepared to continue to act in this way even if they knew that they were a minority and that the majority condemned their actions.

## Irreconcilables and revolutionaries

It is not necessary to dwell for long on the IRA, the Angry Brigade and the various small left-wing parties which are doing all they can to encourage others to challenge the Government and to break laws, indeed to do anything possible to destroy the existing social and political system. The reason why these groups should be noted is that some on the right in British politics and British life believe that but for these 'subversive elements' the problem being looked at in this book would not exist. For them, the law-breakers fall into two groups – a decent, basically patriotic and law-abiding majority who are misled into wrong behaviour by a tiny minority of dedicated revolutionaries.

This is not the place to assess the motives and philosophies of these small groups, but the general attitude of the mass of those who have less respect for the law is not a conscious desire to break up British society. Their behaviour is also perfectly explicable along lines set out above, which examine the failures of government, its softness towards threats of direct action, the lack of confidence in parliamentary decision-making and the nature of some of the laws being passed. It is possible to detect some who occupy a position between the conscious revolutionaries and the many groups who want to see 'the system' work well but are willing to press their own case by forms of direct action. These people in between are those whose frustration is greater and who are open to arguments that 'they', 'the Establishment', are so unfair, so corrupt and so on that any pressure is legitimate. There are people in this category but they are not very important and their existence does not lend support to the theory that all of our troubles can be put down to a Communist conspiracy.

However, all these sections, from the conscious revolutionaries through the more irreconcilable objectors to the various economic pressure groups ending in highly conservative farmers disrupting traffic with their tractors, draw on and exemplify the growing disrespect for traditional authority. The phenomena that have been described so far in this chapter all come on top of a widespread refusal to feel that, because certain leaders say something, it ought to be obeyed. There is a widespread doubt about and even contempt for authority which underlies all the specific phenomena which have been mentioned so far.

## The doubts about authority

The phenomena being described have been commented on widely. Whether it is workers in a factory, students and their professors, children and school teachers or the public and the police, there is less readiness to accept orders or leadership. The explanations vary. Some have attributed this development to declining sanctions. They feel that, if corporal punishment were restored or heavier penalties (including the death penalty), then reasonable obedience would be restored. Others have blamed widespread education which, it is said, has taught people enough to put questions to those above them but not enough to realise the need for an element of hierarchy and responsibility.

The reasons why people are willing to obey or follow leaders are elaborate and difficult to analyse but it is not solely or even chiefly a matter of sanctions. One interesting situation is when all sanctions are removed. Authority has been examined in cases in which entire military units have been captured and when to obey the officers might be to encounter sanctions from the captors. In this situation, some units' internal authority collapsed, while in others from different nationalities discipline remained good or even better than usual.

Looking at the cases where authority declined, it would appear that the reason was lack of a sense of common purpose. In United States units, where there was a mixture of races, people of different pre-American backgrounds and considerable mutual suspicion and tension, discipline collapsed. Where order was best maintained was in units from traditional communities with long-standing loyalties and established social patterns. In universities, authority has been best maintained where there has been a sense of common respect for certain academic standards, the students' desiring to obtain, and the staffs' being willing to help them obtain, the best possible qualifications. Order has broken down in universities and among groups of students who have no longer shared values and had common purposes with the staff. Similarly, industrial authority has been maintained best in countries where recent experience and popular ideology accept that the interests of management and workers have much in common – that success for one benefits the other.

What has happened in Britain has been a decline in the sense of common purpose among the various sections of the society. This has been hastened by the governmental failures that have been so evident over the last two decades. It has been revealed and reinforced by the weakness of governments under pressure. As some groups, by the use of direct action, have won concessions at the expense of others, the sense of common purpose in the society has declined. At the same time, the weakness of Parliament is partly the result of the lack of a clear, popularly accepted doctrine of representative government. As each section can quote some form of democracy or participation that seems to support its case, the old unity in support of parliamentary government (and any clarity about what that concept implies) has declined. Similarly, as laws have embodied political policies rather than moral precepts, it has been easier to view laws as benefiting one group rather than another, again diminishing any sense of a common obligation to obey.

## Conclusion

This is not the place to attempt to set out ways of reversing the decline in a sense of common purpose in the society and in the consequent increase in people's willingness to see society as an orange to be squeezed by those with the strength or the nerve to extract most juice for themselves. But the phenomenon exists and is serious. If it continues, there may be a descent into anarchy, or the public may find it so uncomfortable that they turn to a form of autocracy which will impose its authority, or matters may trickle on in much the same rather dispiriting way that they have done in recent years. But an awareness of the problem and a willingness to analyse it is at least a start in preparing for a solution which would, it is to be hoped, restore a greater degree of respect for authority without resorting to any restrictions of the liberties that used to be an integral part of a society based firmly on the rule of law.

# NOTES

1  See Granada Television, *The State of the Nation : Parliament* (London: Granada Television, 1973), pp. 97–8.

2  J. A. G. Griffith, *Parliamentary Scrutiny of Government Bills* (London: Allen and Unwin, 1974).

# The economic contradictions of democracy

Samuel Brittan

## The conjecture

The conjecture to be discussed in this chapter is that liberal representative democracy suffers from internal contradictions, which are likely to increase in time, and that, on present indications, the system is likely to pass away within the lifetime of people now adult.[1]

This idea has now become commonplace; and any interest it has must lie in the supporting argument. It may help to avoid misunderstanding if I emphasise right at the beginning that there is no such thing as historical inevitability. The point of saying that a house is on fire is to alert the fire brigade, not to sit back and enjoy the blaze. If my reasoning has any elements of validity, it may help to suggest either what can be done to improve the prospects for our type of democracy or, if that cannot be saved, what can be done to ensure that any successor form of government does the minimum of damage to more fundamental values.

In my own case the values which serve as a yardstick are those of an open society, where a large weight is put on both freedom of speech and freedom to choose one's own way of life, in which no group is oppressed or denied the means of subsistence, and in which the use of force and the infliction of pain (whether or not dignified by the name of punishment) is reduced to the feasible minimum. I mention these clichés simply as a reminder of the more basic ends which any political system should serve. On balance, democracy has advanced them; but there is nothing necessary or invariable about the connection.

Two endemic threats to liberal representative democracy are:

(a) the generation of excessive expectations; and
(b) the disruptive effects of the pursuit of group self-interest in the market place.

These two threats are in an obvious sense of the word 'economic'. I do not wish to underplay other kinds of threat, such as those arising from the clash of irreconcilable nationalisms or from other manifestations of the herd impulse and the self-destructive impulse. But sufficient unto a few pages is the evil discussed therein. Any dangers which I have neglected will – unfortunately – serve to strengthen the argument.

Nor is it part of my thesis that even in the economic sphere people are guided purely by self-interest or by the pursuit of self-chosen ends.[2] Such an assumption is the best starting-off ground for dealing with human beings in their dealings *in normal times* outside the circle of their family and close friends. But people are also interested in their own role and status and in the moral legitimacy of the prevailing order. The changes that have taken place in what is acceptable here – to be discussed later in the paper – have, however, served to aggravate rather than ameliorate the economic threats.

The two of these threats mentioned, excessive expectations and the disruptive pursuit of group self-interest, have different origins. Excessive expectations are generated by the democratic aspects of the system. The disruptive effects of group self-interest arise from elementary economic logic and are not directly connected with the political structure.

Nevertheless, the 'liberal' aspect of liberal representative democracy is important as an inhibition on tackling the group pursuit of market power. Some 'People's Democracies' and some trigger-happy military dictatorships (by no means all) have shown that they can deal, at a price, with coercive power of rival groups. But it has yet to be shown that a society where legislation can be enforced only if it enjoys at least the tacit long-run acceptance of all major groups, including those on the losing side, can do so. The omens are not good.

There are clear interrelations between the two problems – the pursuit of group self-interest and the generation of excessive expectations in the political market place. Producer groups, of which the trade unions are an outstanding but by no means unique example, have not in the past made use of their full potential power, but have tended to make increasing use of it as time has passed. It is commonplace to observe that the size of group demands depends on members' expectations; but these in turn have been fanned by the competitive wooing of the electorate. Moreover, as already implied, liberal democracy inhibits governments from tackling coercive groups either by an abnegation of the full employment commitment, or by the effective restriction of union monopoly power, or by the enforcement of an 'incomes policy'.

A formula which may link the two problems is that an *excessive burden is placed on the 'sharing out' function of government*.[3] This function may be defined as the activities of the public authorities in influencing the allocation of resources, both through taxation and expenditure policies and through direct intervention in the market place. The growth of expectations imposes demands for different kinds of public spending and intervention which are incompatible both with each other and with the tax burden that people are willing to bear. At the same time, in their pursuit of 'full employment' without currency collapse, governments are tempted to intervene directly in the determination of pre-tax incomes. But these attempts come to grief when they come up against the demands of different groups for incompatible relative shares.

The tensions described here are at work in most countries, but they need not have the same outcome in different places. The fact that they are particularly acute in the U.K., which provides the case material for this study, is shown by the use of the label 'English sickness' when they turn up elsewhere. The question is left open in this chapter whether the *dénouement* will be more favourable to liberal democracy in some other countries than the U.K. The greater tradition of stability in the British case has to be balanced against the greater severity of the pressures. But the view is taken here that the stresses are those endemic to democracy everywhere and were already visible before the world oil crisis, which of course made them more difficult to bear.

## The political market place

To carry the analysis further, it is necessary to put forward some view, inevitably brief and oversimplified, of the nature of liberal representative democracy.

The 'liberal' part of the label refers to the standard civil liberties of expression, association and assembly, together with the generally accepted constraints upon the degree of coercion which the forces of government can impose upon dissidents. I have in mind not some ideal free or open society,[4] but the degree of tolerance and personal freedom which Western countries normally expect to achieve, and lapses from which give rise to criticism and anxiety.

A good deal more needs to be said about the 'representative democracy' aspects of the system. My starting-off point is Schumpeter's theory. Schumpeter defined democracy as an 'institutional arrangement for arriving at political decisions in which individuals acquire the power to decide by means of a competitive struggle for the people's votes'.[5] There is a link between the 'liberal' and the 'democratic' aspects of the system thus defined, but it is a loose one. If rival political teams are to compete, a minimal freedom of debate is required; and, once freedom has acquired a toehold in the party political arena, it tends to spread to wider areas. Yet it is essential to remember the distinction between the two aspects. The link is loose enough to allow persecution of unpopular minorities and widespread restraints upon freedom of action in systems with unfettered elections and majority decisions. Indeed such repressive actions have been common in democracies – though less widespread (in modern times at least) than in undemocratic regimes.

The point of Schumpeter's theory becomes clear when we compare it with the popular theory[6] which assumes that electors have definite beliefs about policy, represented by political parties which are expected to implement them. Edmund Burke defined a political party as a group of men who intend to promote the public welfare upon some principles upon which they are all agreed. In subsequent forms of the popular theory, parties were actually expected to formulate their policies in response to the desires of their mass membership.

Such models of democracy received a body blow when nineteenth-century writers such as Michels, Mosca and Pareto showed that no mass democracy could or did work in this way. Policies were formulated by small groups within political parties or the civil service; and what was done often had very little relation to professed ideologies. These sceptical conclusions were confirmed very much later by sophisticated opinion studies pioneered by the 'Michigan School', which showed that most voters were largely oblivious of most policy debates in the legislature and the press.[7] The strongest claim that can be made on behalf of voters' awareness is that they do have a rough general impression of the stands of the main parties on a few of the headline issues when these are sufficiently simple.

The lesson of most studies of electoral choice is that changes in political allegiance are more performance-related than issue-related (although the distinction may be one of degree). Voters attempt to judge success in the pursuit of generally agreed objectives, such as peace or prosperity, rather than to evaluate rival objectives or alternative policies for achieving agreed objectives. The studies show that, not merely do voters not use the labels 'left' or 'right', they do not think in such terms at all. To the extent that most people think in terms of issues at all, their attitudes are largely atomistic. On many issues on which the official positions of the parties are sharply divided, the proportion of people supporting different policies bears almost no relation to partisan allegiance. Clusters or 'ideologies', linking together opinions on different issues among the politically interested minority, are almost completely absent among the mass electorate. Such refusal to conform to stereotype is due not to nonconformist heresy, but much more often to basic ignorance of the simplest facts taken for granted even in the most popular of newspapers or television programmes. Voters simplify the problems of choice by shifting attention from policies to consequences; beliefs about the latter are formed by 'simple inferences from who is or was in power'.[8]

Schumpeter's achievement was to show that representative democracy could work and need not be a fraud, despite these features. The best way to think of politicians, he maintained, was neither as ideologues nor as spokesmen, but as entrepreneurs who deal in votes just as oilmen deal in oil. The principles or policy platforms which characterise a political party may be important for its success at a given moment, but they have no deeper or more permanent significance than the particular brand lines that a department store finds it expedient to carry this month but may well want to change next spring or autumn. Different department stores will feel more at home with different kinds of merchandise, but all will alter their lines in trial and error fashion in a bid to win public support. More deep-seated divergences are to be viewed as pathological symptoms.

Like all good theories, this is an unrealistic simplification. But it is neither as cynical nor as shocking as it appears at first sight. It is the political equivalent of Adam Smith's doctrine that it is not from the benevolence of the butcher, the brewer or the baker that we expect our dinner, but from their regard to their own interest. In politics as in economics, the pursuit of self-interest may, contrary to what unreflective moralists suppose, serve to promote the welfare of one's fellow citizens.

## Excessive expectations

Schumpeter's own criterion for the success of a political system was fairly modest. By success he did not mean achieving an ideal, being on a Pareto optimum or anything of that kind, but simply that it could reproduce itself without creating conditions which led to resort to undemocratic methods, or – which he took to be equivalent – that all major interests would in the long run abide by the results of the democratic process.

He himself was non-committal on democracy's prospects. But his own analysis provides plenty of grounds to expect a trend towards excessive expectations, which could prove fatal. Unlike his more formal successors who have elaborated on his competitive model,[9] he did not hesitate to draw on the analysis of crowd psychology.[10] People in a crowd are apt to exhibit a reduced sense of responsibility and a lower level of energy and thought than the same individuals in their private or business life. A crowd need not mean a screaming mob in a sultry city. It can just as easily be a television audience, or electorate, or a committee of generals in their 60s. Even supposedly individual demands are not the outcome of rational deliberation about the best means of satisfying inherent desires but can be artificially generated by advertising or propaganda.

These anti-rational or non-rational influences are less important in personal, business or professional life than in political behaviour. Frequently repeated experience in everyday life, as well as personal responsibility, exert a rationalising influence. 'The picture of the prettiest girl that ever lived will in the long run prove powerless to maintain the sales of a bad cigarette.'[11] Failure to take this on board accounts for the vast overemphasis by Galbraith on the powers of a large firm to manipulate consumer demand.

The rationalising influence of personal experience can be extended to hobbies, relations with friends, the affairs of a small township or a small social group. It might also influence views on public policy where personal pecuniary matters are at stake. But here the influence acts mainly in favour of influencing short-run rationality and short-run aims. Schumpeter's most telling comparison is that of the attitude of the lawyer to his brief to the same lawyer's attitude to political statements in his newspaper. In the first instance he has not only the competence, but also the stimulus, to master the material. In the latter he is 'not all there' morally or intellectually. Without the pressures that come from personal responsibility, masses of information and education will not help, and he 'will not apply the canons of criticism he knows so well how to handle' in his own sphere.[12] For most people the great political issues are 'sub-hobbies' to which they devote less attention than to bridge; and there is little check either on dark urges or on bursts of general indignation.

The more modern 'economic' analysis of rational political behaviour also leads to the conclusion that it is irrational to be rational, because of the information and other costs involved. This is highlighted by the problem of the *voting paradox*, that is the problem of finding a self-interested motive for voting when the probability of any one vote determining the outcome is vanishingly small. Its importance is not the literal one of explaining why most electors vote. The cost of so doing is extremely small; and a sense of public duty, emotional satisfaction or a blown-up sense of self-importance can be called in aid. The validity of the phenomenon to which it refers can be seen by the way in which the slightest increase in the cost of voting influences the turnout. A U.S. Presidential Commission, for example, called in aid such extremely simple practices as voting on a Sunday to explain part of the difference between turnouts of 80–92 per cent in German and Italian national elections and U.S. presidential turnouts of little more than 60 per cent.[13] In the

U.K., Labour party leaders, who face the greatest risk of abstention, have been known to protest against the possible appearance on polling night of popular television serials.

The main point is that, if a self-interested citizen has little or no incentive to vote, he has even less to make a detailed study of facts, controversies and policies. Any short cut, such as taking on trust views of the party one generally supports, or going by television impressions, will be quite rationally undertaken to avoid time-consuming study, which would in any case hardly be feasible over more than a very tiny range. Given the likely extent of individual influence, it is perfectly reasonable to regard political programmes as show business, to be watched only if they are entertaining.

Nor is such reasoning applicable just to non-political citizens. An individual MP has such a small chance of influencing his party's policy that it is rational for him to use short-cut methods, such as following a particular leader or faction within his party, on all except a handful of issues of which he has made a speciality. It is on these lines that one can best explain the role of stereotyped packages of ideas or ideologies. A politician, civil servant or academic who has neither the time nor the incentive to study every subject in depth can reasonably ask : 'From what stable does this particular idea come?' It may be better than going by pure hunch.

These considerations would not themselves be a threat to democracy if they simply led to the wrong result in particular elections or in particular policy decisions. The basic trouble is *the lack of a budget constraint among voters*. This means that errors are biased in a particular direction. In their own private lives, people know that more of one thing means less of something else, on a given income and capital. They know that they can improve the tradeoffs, such as that between take-home pay and leisure, by a careful choice of residence. But they also know that such improvements are not unlimited and cost effort to find. In the absence of such knowledge in the political sphere, electorates tend to expect too much from government action at too little cost, e.g. a painless improvement in economic growth or reduction in inflation, and they tend both to praise and blame governments for things which are largely outside their control. The impetus to consistency, without the discipline and responsibility of personal experience, is not strong.

The temptation to encourage false expectations among the electorate becomes overwhelming to politicians. The opposition parties are bound to promise to do better and the government party must join in the auction – explaining away the past and outbidding its rivals for the future, whether by general hints or detailed promises. Voters may indeed be cynical about promises. An NOP poll taken in the late summer of 1974 showed 68 per cent 'not very' or 'not at all confident' that the present political parties could solve Britain's problems,[14] and well over 50 per cent thought that *both* main parties were 'making promises which the country cannot afford'.[15] Yet citizens' demands for government action and their attribution to it of responsibility for their own or the nation's past performance are altogether excessive.

The analogy with commercial advertisements, which promise to fulfill all our daydreams if we buy 'getaway' petrol or the right type of underwear, is inescapable; the difference is the absence of the immediate and personal corrective experience. The elector cannot compare experimentally a wide range of different governments and policies and examine their effects in isolation from other disturbing influences. Moreover, the normal competitive processes tend to bring to the top within each party leaders who genuinely believe that they can improve the tradeoffs more than is actually possible – usually by some form of minor improvement in machinery of administration. The obvious British examples were Harold Wilson and Edward Heath both of whom attached disproportionate weight to Whitehall reorganisation, both in their initial plans while in opposition and in their first years of power. Such attitudes are perfectly compatible with a great deal of apparent tough talking but do not suit the sceptic or realist who actually knows the score.

The expectations that are relevant are not all the wants and demands that people make of life, but only those expectations which they expect the political process to underwrite. These expectations can be shown *ex ante* in positive if vaguely formulated demands, and *ex post* in the attribution of blame for events and developments. A report by the Survey Research Unit of the Social Science Research Council[16] showed that 67 per cent of respondents felt in 1973 that their standard of living was below the one to which they were entitled. The average respondent felt that he was entitled to a standard of living 20 per cent more than he actually had. But there was a large spread round this average. The most modest aspirations were held by 'the rich, the very poor and the elderly'. Most other sections felt that they needed an extra £8 or £9 a week (in end-1973 pounds). The behaviour of politicians in the year subsequent to the survey showed that they were very sensitive to such aspirations. Although they called for 'sacrifices' on account of inflation and oil crises, they were extremely reluctant to take any measures which might reduce consumption. Indeed the action of the Labour Government in freezing the rents of council tenants, from whom it expected to draw a large vote, and of the Conservatives in promising '9½ per cent mortgages' at a time of rapidly rising prices, showed that they were still in the game of whipping up expectations among different groups.

I am not pretending, of course, to offer a complete theory of political expectations, which are determined by innumerable forces apart from competitive vote-bidding. The spread of information about other people's life styles through the media and advertising, so that they look like attainable ideals rather than fantasies, is frequently cited. The breakdown of traditional ideas of hierarchy, to be discussed below, is another obvious influence. It has also been suggested that expectations tend to be low during protracted periods of

106

economic hardship, as they were in the depression of the 1930s; the gap between expectation and reality is greater during periods of prosperity and advance, and perhaps greatest of all when expectations are frustrated by a sudden and unexpected check to progress.[17] The main point to stress is that democracy, viewed as a process of political competition, itself imparts a systematic upward bias to expectations and compounds the other influences at work.

Is it possible that the gap between expectations and performance will ultimately prove self-correcting as public credibility becomes eroded? There are certainly periods of masochistic reaction in which parties vie with each other in promising hard times ahead. The periodic revulsions towards 'sweat, toil and tears' are, however, no more rational than the conventional outbidding. Each person is concerned that others should bear their proper share of sacrifice and that 'less essential' activities should be cut down to size. It is still likely that, if we could add up the demands by different people for their own groups and their own favoured section of public expenditure, the result would far exceed the resources available.

It is interesting, too, that moves away from excessive promises have so far taken the form only of hesitation about promising a larger cake. The outbidding continues on promises about distribution. Unfortunately, neither promises of redistribution from politicians nor demands for it from the electorate carry with them a knowledge of how much there is to redistribute, let alone a consensus on a just distribution. In the early spring of 1974, after a general election in which the Labour and Liberal parties had fought on a platform of redistribution and the Conservatives on 'fairness and firmness', a poll showed that only a third of those asked were willing to pay more taxes 'to help people who do not earn so much money as yourself'.[18]

The elector tends, because he has no yardstick in his everyday life against which to measure consistency, to favour all worthy objects at the same time : more of the national in-

107

come for the old and sick, the lower paid, the skilled crafts-man, for those doing important professional work, the mort-gagee, the ratepayer, and so on. The one group which people always think too well paid are the politicians, from whom omnipotence and omniscience are expected.

Nor are distribution and growth *per se* the only sphere in which excessive demands are made from the political pro-cess. The U.S. administration is expected to prevent pollution without increasing transportation or energy costs, to protect forests and lower timber prices – and in general to protect the environment – without paying any obvious price. What has gone is the tacit belief in limiting the role of political decision : and this is likely to put a burden on democratic procedures which they are not designed to bear. The useful-ness of inflationary finance as a short-term method of post-poning political choice between incompatible objectives has long been known. By running a budget deficit, financed by excess money creation and rationalised by some fashionable economic theory, government is able for a time to increase some expenditures without curtailing others or increasing taxes overtly. (The citizen of course pays through the 'tax' that inflation levies on the value of his nominal income and monetary assets.) But enormously important though it may be, inflation is but a particular case of the consequences of inconsistent expectations and demands.

*The rivalry of coercive groups*

It has already been suggested that the pursuit of group self-interest through coercive means in the market place is a much more serious threat to democracy than the traditional log-rolling among legislators and ministers. The most obvious form of this is the conflict of different groups of trade unionists – ostensibly with the government or employers, but in reality with each other – for shares of the national product. This rivalry induces more and more sections of the popula-tion, including those who have previously relied on individualist efforts, into militant trade unionist attitudes in self-defence.

The direct effect of unions is not, as is popularly believed, to cause a continuing inflation. This cannot happen without an accompanying expansion of monetary demand. The contribution of unions to inflation is indirect. First, if a sufficient number of trade unionists make *increased* use of their monopoly power, this leads to a loss of jobs for their members, and also for other people, to the extent that more purchasing power is absorbed in the purchase of the output of the strongly unionised sector. As those displaced will be slow to accept reduced real wages or to price themselves into other (and in their eyes inferior) jobs, the net result will be an increase in the unemployment total. Inflation comes into the picture when governments expand the money supply and increase their budget deficits in an attempt to mop up the unemployment by pushing more spending money into the economy. But this by its nature can be, at best, of only temporary assistance. For unless the stronger unions are indefinitely fooled by the 'money illusion', they will demand and receive further wage increases to restore the differentials which their original settlements were intended to achieve. This in turn will threaten unemployment and tempt or force governments into a further expansion of monetary demand and a repetition of the earlier process. As the spiral proceeds, the result is not inflation, but accelerating inflation. In the last analysis the authorities have to choose between accepting an indefinite increase in the rate of inflation and abandoning full employment to the extent necessary to break the collective wage-push power of the unions.[19]

Even in the absence of such a politico-economic spiral, there is a second way in which the unions can make the control of inflation prohibitively difficult. Let us assume that the rate of inflation has reached, for reasons unconnected with the unions, a level which has become politically, socially and commercially intolerable. To move to a lower rate will require a slowdown in the growth of spending brought about through tighter fiscal and monetary policies. How far and how soon this slowdown is reflected in smaller rises in money incomes and prices, and how far it is wasted in increased unemployment, will depend on the extent to which unions resist the forces of the labour market and price their members out of jobs.

If this resistance is very strong, governments may still have to choose between very high rates of unemployment and very high rates of inflation, neither of which can be sustained by a liberal democracy. The conjecture of Peter Jay, the Economics Editor of the London *Times*, that 'free' collective bargaining, full employment and a usable currency are not in the long run mutually compatible has never been convincingly answered; nor has his conjecture that a liberal democracy is unlikely to be able to abandon any one of the three.[20]

Union monopolies differ in an important way from other organised groups. A business monopoly, or cartel with market power, will hold its output below competitive levels for the sake of higher prices. A farmers' association will try to achieve the same effect by political lobbying. But none of these will normally withdraw output from the market until representatives of the public sign an agreement to pay more. This is a quasi-political power or threat, different in many ways from the textbook monopoly. Of course, there have been collective boycotts and even a resort to violence in business history, especially in the U.S. in the late nineteenth century, but nothing as extended in scale or as pervasive throughout the economy as the effects of union power in the context of a commitment to full employment.

There have been numerous proposals, dating back in embryo to the 1944 Employment White Paper, that demand management should seek to stabilise the growth of expenditure in money terms in line with the growth of productive potential. In that case the unions would know that the faster money wages rose the fewer jobs there would be. The same logic is inherent in the principle of a fixed annual target for

110

the growth of the money supply, and lay behind Peter Thorneycroft's pronouncement as Chancellor in the short period between his measures of September 1957 and his resignation over 'little local difficulties' early the following January.[21]

The trouble with such policies is that they have only deterrent value; they might work if they carried credibility, but risk collapse if the threat has to be used. To take by no means fanciful illustrative figures, let us imagine that a limit of 10 per cent per annum is set to the growth of nominal income and expenditure but that wage settlements, in conjunction with normal pricing procedures, require a growth of 20 per cent if unemployment is to be held constant and output to grow by a normal amount. What then is to be done? A reduction of output of nearly 10 per cent at the end of a single year of the policy, with whatever rise in unemployment that goes with it, will normally appear too large a price to pay. Until the spectre of hyperinflation and currency breakdown – perhaps disguised as a mammoth foreign exchange crisis – finally arrives, the monetary and fiscal targets will be the main ones to give way; and participants in wage bargaining are well aware of this. Each group of union negotiators knows that most other groups are pushing for wage increases; and the risk of its being left behind the others is greater than that of the monetary authorities' refusing to finance the result.

The conventional answer to this demand is that a voluntary or statutory 'incomes policy' could modify collective bargaining enough to prevent governments from being faced with such impossible choices. Now even if a long-term statutory incomes policy could resolve this dilemma – and this is not the place to discuss whether it could and at what price – it is unenforceable for any extended period if democracy is to remain 'liberal' and violent means of coercion are not to be employed on dissenting groups. (Indeed, if public opinion is in this sense 'liberal', then it is unenforceable so long as democracy of any sort prevails.) Thus the only sort of incomes policy that could help would be a voluntary one, or at least a statutory one that enjoyed the 'full-hearted consent' of those affected by it. Apart from brief emergency freezes, the main problem posed by such a policy is one of relativities, as every schoolboy knows.

Agreement on such relativities is extremely unlikely on any self-interested basis. The basic difficulty is that the benefits from restraint in the use of group market power are 'public goods'. They consist of things such as price stability, fuller employment or faster economic growth, which are thinly diffused among the whole population, while the costs are incurred by the group which exercises restraint. It is therefore in the interest of each union group that other unions should show restraint while it exploits its own mono-poly power to the full. For it is clear to any particular union leader that most of the gains from price stability and fuller employment spill over to members of other unions and the general public, while the costs of settling for less than he could obtain are highly concentrated among his own mem-bers. The chances that an example of restraint by one will be followed by others is so small that his best bet is to pursue his members' own interests. If the leadership of a union is prepared to look beyond the (fairly short-term) self-interest of its own members, it is likely eventually to be thrown out of office. One does not have to look for 'reds under the bed'. The 'militant moderates' will do the job; and rationally so from the members' point of view.

It is uncertain whether the unions are unique in the role they exercise. A possible comparison is the fivefold increase in the oil price made by the OPEC countries in 1973–74. If this was a once-for-all event, the analogy does not hold. For however severe the initial disruption, it could not push the world monetary authorities into policies of continuously accelerating inflation. If, on the other hand, there are going to be further attempts by producers to raise the price of oil (relative to other commodities) by withholding supplies, or if similar cartels are to be formed among other primary producers, and if in turn industrial workers are going to strike in an attempt to preserve their relative share of world income, then the analogy will hold and the problem becomes the wider one of the explosive potentialities of certain means of pursuing group interest. On present evidence, however, the problem focuses on union power in an environment of high labour demand.

Indeed the difficulties that unions pose for anti-inflationary policy are but the surface manifestations of a much more fundamental threat posed by the rivalry of coercive groups; that is, that they are likely to have non-negotiable demands for more than a country's whole output. Such demands risk straining to breaking point what has been termed the 'sharing out' function of democratic society. The paradox that the freedom of individuals to form associations can itself threaten individual freedom was noted by A. V. Dicey as early as 1905.[22] What is true for freedom is also true in the economic field. While the individual pursuit of self-interest within a framework of rules and conventions is compatible with the successful functioning of a market economy, the group pursuit of self-interest may be inherently unstable. Even if the government could in the circumstances still pursue a non-inflationary monetary policy, the conflicts and instability would still be there. Indeed a non-inflationary policy would bring them more quickly into the open, which is one reason why it is so rarely pursued.

It is sometimes asserted that the explosive potentialities from the collective pursuit of self-interest are due to the new vulnerability of a modern economy to group action which did not previously exist. But it is often forgotten that as long ago as 17 July 1914 Lloyd George declared that if the threats of the Irish Rebellion and the Triple Industrial Alliance were to materialise, 'the situation will be the gravest with which any government has had to deal for centuries'.[23] Ernest Bevin subsequently said of these events : 'It was a period which, if the war had not broken out, would have, I believe, seen one of the greatest revolts the world would ever have seen.'[24]

## The vanishing heritage

The mention of earlier alarms brings us to one of the main problems facing the analysis so far presented. This is why the tensions endemic to democracy did not emerge much earlier than they have. We have no lack of warnings about the self-destructive tendencies of democracy dating back well into the nineteenth century. Bagehot's Introduction to the Second Edition of *The English Constitution*, written after the 1867 Reform Bill, is full of gloomy forebodings about the effects of enfranchising an ignorant and greedy electorate, and full of fury with Disraeli for having sold the pass.[25] While preparing this chapter, I came across a remarkable address given by the historian J. A. Froude to the 'Liberty and Property Defence League' in 1887.[26] Some of the passages could have been reproduced without alteration in the political and fiscal debates of 1974.

Writing in the aftermath of the Third Reform Bill, Froude warned :

> It is one man one vote. And as the poor and the ignorant are the majority, I think it is perfectly certain – and it is only consistent with all one has ever heard or read of human nature – that those who have the power will use it to bring about what they consider to be a more equitable distribution of the good things of this world.

Some egalitarians will claim that this quotation gives the game away and that all the doom-mongering from Bagehot and Froude down to the present day simply reflects the fear of the rich and the powerful that they will lose their favoured position. The attribution of a motive does not, however, make the content of the warnings groundless. If 'a more equitable division' were an unproblematic and costless operation, we could afford to dismiss the warnings. But there

114

are both historical and logical reasons for agreeing with Froude, that the result of attempts to bring about such a division has always been and always will be : 'factions and quarrels, confiscation and civil disturbances, and the convulsions of war . . . and finally an end to liberty'.

A good insight into the forces by which liberal democracy has so far protected itself against the tensions proclaimed by the doom-mongers can be obtained by going back to Schumpeter and re-examining some of the conditions he set for the effective working of the system. The most important was that *the effective range of political decision should not be extended too far*.[27] Most issues are too complex to be decided by a competitive vote-seeking process. Although parliament may vote on such issues and ministers may introduce legislation, their actions are purely formal, as the real decisions will have been made elsewhere. This applies not only to issues such as the permissible size of the budget deficit or official operations in the foreign exchange market but to as fundamental a matter as the criminal code, which would otherwise be at the mercy of alternating fits of vindictiveness and sentimentality.

Schumpeter makes a very firm distinction between extending the area of state authority and extending the area of political decision. The former can be done by means of agencies whose heads are not appointed by competition for votes and who do not have to please the electorate in any direct or immediate sense. Apart from the permanent civil service, there are many special agencies whose non-political nature is constantly stressed both by themselves and by the government of the day. Perhaps the most interesting historical example is the pre-1914 Bank of England which made key economic policy decisions at its own discretion. There are numerous regulatory agencies in the U.S. which, if they are influenced by anyone, are influenced by the industries they are supposed to regulate. In Britain we have long had experience of organisations such as the BBC, the University Grants Committee and the Morrisonian public corporation.

It is no coincidence that bodies such as the Prices and Incomes Board, the Pay and Prices Board and *ad hoc* committees presided over by judges have been used to extend state control into the most sensitive areas of economic life.

Another vital condition put forward by Schumpeter for the success of a competitive vote-bidding system was *tolerance and democratic self-control.*[28] All groups must be willing to accept legislation on the statute book. Political warfare must be kept within certain limits; and this involves the cabinet and shadow cabinet being followed by their supporters and not being pushed from behind. Political action is to be left to politicians without too much back-seat driving, let alone direct action. We cannot expect to see these conditions met unless the main interests are agreed on the broad structure of society. If the electorate is divided into two or more deeply hostile camps, or there are rival ideals on which no compromise is possible, these restraints will cease to function and democracy may wither.

A further requirement was *the existence of a well-trained bureaucracy*[29] – not the powerless eunuch of constitutional mythology, but a group with their own principles not merely of procedure, but in a more subtle sense of policy as well, deciding on their own promotions and enjoying security of tenure. Many people would say that we have such a class, which has been responsible for our major postwar blunders and for preventing both Labour and Conservative Governments from implementing distinctive policies of their own, and that this has led to a proliferation of ideas for introducing irregulars, outsiders, ministerial *cabinets*, 'think tanks' and so on, the results of which have been – to put it mildly – not spectacular.

The reason why an entrenched bureaucracy is so essential is precisely because politicians are professionals at dealing in votes but amateurs both in administration and in policy-making, with a strong tendency (already discussed) to take refuge in the world of the advertising slogan and the media headline; in other words, the alleged orthodoxy and lack of imagination of the bureaucrat is part of the price of having a democratic system at all.

But without the fulfilment of the earlier conditions – a limit on the area of political decision and a sufficient agreement on the broad structure of society to enable groups to accept legislation with which they disagree – such a professional bureaucracy will not function effectively and its morale and effectiveness will be undermined, as they manifestly have been in the U.K. since the mid-1960s. Evidence for the frustrations felt by senior civil servants is the plaintive demand frequently made in conversation (and hinted at in the Queen's Speech of March 1974) that certain officials should be assigned the job of advising the opposition, so that it does not come to office so ill-prepared. (One very prominent official not long ago observed privately that he would like to be on holiday for the first two years after every change of government!)

Mass electorates were able to accept the Schumpeter conditions of self-restraint for a surprisingly long period partly because they were slow to realise their power. The lack of incentives for the voter to inform himself has already been emphasised. There were also a series of *ad hoc* events such as the First World War, which produced an external threat and a patriotic myth to override sectional conflicts, and the Great Depression, which weakened the market-power of the trade unions.

But just as important was an ethic, which took a long time to erode, which limited the demands on the sharing out functions of the state. As Kristol has emphasised,[30] personal success was seen by nineteenth-century defenders of capitalism as having a firm connection with 'duty performed'. In a society 'still permeated by a Puritan ethic' it

> was agreed that there was a strong correlation between certain personal virtues – frugality, industry, sobriety, reliability, piety – and the way in which power, privilege and property were distributed. And this correlation was

taken to be the sign of a just society, not merely a free one. Samuel Smiles or Horatio Alger would have regarded Professor Hayek's writings [divorcing reward from merit] as slanderous of his fellow Christians, blasphemous of God, and ultimately subversive of the social order.[31]

The point that Kristol does not bring out sufficiently is that the public morality of early capitalist bourgeois society was a transitional one. On its own grounds it could not hope to stand up to serious analysis. Luck was even then as important as merit in the gaining of awards, and merit was inherently a subjective concept in the eye of the beholder. Hayek is right not to base his defence of a market economy upon it.[32] Early capitalist civilisation was living on the moral heritage of the feudal system under which each man had a superior to whom he owed obligations and from whom he received protection in a 'great chain of duties'. A medieval king was expected to 'do justice and to render each his due'. It was not a matter of what the king thought a subject ought to have, or what the subject thought best for himself, but what belonged to him according to custom, which in turn was supported by theological sanction.

For a long time capitalist civilisation was able to live on this feudal legacy, and the aura of legitimacy was transferred from the feudal lord to the employer, from the medieval hierarchy of position to that derived from the luck of the market place. But this feudal legacy was bound to be extinguished by the torchlight of secular and rationalistic inquiry, which was itself so closely associated with the rise of capitalism. The personal qualities of middle-class leaders did not help to kindle that affection for the social order which is probably necessary if it is not to be blamed for the inevitable tribulations and disappointments of most people's lives. Modern politicians and business chiefs lack the glamour of an aristocracy. With neither the trappings of tradition nor the heroic qualities of great war leaders or generals, they cannot excite the identification or hero worship which previously reconciled people to much greater differences of wealth and position than exist today. Moreover, the 'fairer' the process of selection, the less the governing classes are differentiated by special clothes or accents, the more they will be resented. At most they are tolerated on the strict condition that they bring results; and we have seen that expectations here tend to be excessive.

Schumpeter himself had some half-hearted hopes that the degree of institutional consensus and agreement on fundamentals required for the working of democracy might be restored under 'socialism'. For one thing, the issue of capitalism *versus* socialism would be out of the way, and there would be no more argument about profits, dividends, private ownership of capital or gains from rising land values. Moreover, the twentieth-century development of non-political agencies made socialism possible and perhaps compatible with democracy. By 'socialism' he had in mind the old-fashioned definition of collective control over the means of production – roughly the 'Clause 4' conception. But the condition of success was that democratic politics was *not* extended to economic affairs. Beyond setting the rules in the most general way possible, it was essential that politicians resist the temptation to interfere with the activities of the managers of state enterprises and regulatory boards. (He had in mind a form of market socialism on Lange-Lerner lines.) Indeed Schumpeter remarked that at long last managers would be able to do their jobs without guilt-feelings and with more freedom not only from interfering politicians but also from fussing committees of consumers, demands for workers' control and all other demands for 'participation'.

We do not, however, need to follow out these paradoxes, because the type of collectivism now in vogue among all parties concerns not only ownership of productive assets but also, and more important, relative incomes. The popular desire is to transfer from the private to the public sphere the determination of who gets how much; and to make this determination neither on the basis of market values, nor egalitarian principles, nor some compromise between them, but by a revival of the medieval notion of the just wage – a doctrine sometimes miscalled 'fairness'. This is to be done, moreover, without benefit of the feudal relationships and scholastic theology which enabled an earlier age to attach a meaning to such concepts.

It is hardly conceivable that anything as sensitive as the determination of relative rewards will be left to bodies enjoying the degree of autonomy of the pre-1914 Bank of England or the nationalised industries before their finances and freedom were undermined by prices and incomes policy. Reference has already been made to bodies such as the Pay Board which may occasionally provide politicians with a useful fig leaf. But if pre-tax incomes are to be determined, or even heavily influenced, by state authority, elected politicians will want – quite rightly – to have the last word; and their decisions are bound to figure prominently in the competitive struggle for votes – again rightly so. Thus currently fashionable doctrines, so far from providing a solvent for the tensions of democracy, seem likely to make them worse.

## The argument so far

It might at this stage be worth giving a provisional summary of the argument of the chapter. Democratic political practice is best regarded neither as a method of popular participation in government nor as a means of putting into effect the people's will, but mainly as a competition for power by means of votes among competing teams. But, even when viewed in this relatively unambitious light, it is subject to endemic and growing weaknesses. The two principal ones analysed in the preceding pages are the generation of excessive expectations among voters by the processes of political competition and the disruptive effects arising from the pursuit of self-interest by rival coercive groups. These weaknesses have become more important than they were before because of the lack of any widely shared belief in the legitimacy of the present order, which might have held them in check. Nor, on the other hand, is there any commonly held conception of any feasible alternative social order in which democracy might operate in the future.

The diagnosis, if true, has grave consequences not only for democracy and freedom of action but also for intellectual freedom and freedom of speech. This was originally defended by its great expositors from Milton to Mill as a means towards the discovery of truth. But let us suppose, in line with much modern thinking, that there is no absolute truth on fundamentals of morals and politics or, if there is, that it cannot easily be found. A free society will then produce in de Jouvenel's words, not a convergence but a divergence with 'less and less agreement on the general rules of social life, with each sect seeking to make its respective principles the criterion'.[33]

If the divergences are strongly felt and far-reaching, de Jouvenel points to three consequences which will follow. First, the laws must be tightly enforced to prevent society tearing itself apart. To do this requires a repressive force since citizens are not united by any belief, not even belief in legality. But, secondly, 'laws which are at stake in embittered public conflicts do not inspire much respect, even among those who execute them'. It would, therefore, be tempting to entrust the making of laws to some authority outside the public arena. Even this, however, would not be enough. For 'institutions cannot maintain themselves in being forever without consent'. The third temptation would, therefore, be to strike at disorder at its source, and for the rulers to do their best to prevent the dispersion and clash of opinion – e.g. expel Solzhenitsyn from the polity – thereby reducing the need to rely on police repression.[34]

It is by such reasoning that de Jouvenel convincingly explains the link between Hobbes's extreme individualism – in which no one desire can be regarded as higher or better than any other – and his ultimate authoritarianism. But any number of other big names have traced in only slightly differing forms the path from extreme individualism to the extinction of freedom. There was Dostoevsky's parable of the grand inquisitor, or Rousseau's insistence on silence on the part of philosophers in his ideal democratic society.

## *The mirage of social justice*

It should by this time be obvious that a resolution of the problems of liberal democracy is unlikely on a basis relying entirely on self-interest or private-interest (which need not be selfish in the vulgar sense). Can any other motives be brought in which would both make members of economic groups refrain from exercising their full market power and induce electors to reduce the excessive and incompatible demands they make on government services? Is it possible to create or evolve a consensus, so far missing, on a legitimate social order which would appeal to people's sense of justice and persuade them to moderate their pursuit of private interest, both in the ballot box and in their other collective activities?

The problems discussed would clearly be a good deal easier if there was some consensus on how goods, status and power should be shared out. The common view that the basis of consent at present missing could be supplied by the pursuit of 'social justice' or 'fairness' is in all probability fallacious. At its most primitive level such thinking assumes that 'social justice' and 'fairness' are natural qualities such as redness or hardness, which are either present or not. Some more sophisticated exponents of this approach realise that subjective nature of such concepts and try to seek a *de facto* consensus. But there is in fact little agreement on what *ought* to determine relative income levels, let alone wider matters of power, opportunity, prestige or influence. As a leading sociologist has written, 'Given the diversity of moral positions that are tenable in the existing state of public opinion, virtually any occupational group seeking a pay increase is likely to be able to find some legitimization for pressing its case.'[35] Hence the proliferation of incompatible criteria: rewarding skill, overcoming labour shortages, helping the lower paid, preserving traditional differentials and so on.

There are two logically tenable ways of looking at the distribution of resources. One is to envisage a pie, to be divided up by a central authority. From this point of view, the natural principle of division is equality and departures from it have to be justified. The other is to emphasise that

> we are not in the position of children who have been given some portions of pie . . . There is no central distribution. What each person gets, he gets from others who give it to him in exchange for something, or as a gift. In a free society, diverse persons control different resources, and new holdings arise out of the voluntary exchange and actions of persons . . . The total result is the product of many individual decisions.[36]

Provided that the initial holdings were justly acquired, there can be no question of social injustice or wrongful distribution – although there may still be a desire to help the worst off for humanitarian reasons.

The two approaches may be called the entitlement theory and the pie theory. The weakness of the entitlement theory is that the very content of property rights and the rules governing their transfer, as well as their physical protection, are the result of collectively enforced rules and decisions, which we are at liberty to change. As Froude put it, 'Without the State there would be no such thing as property. The State guarantees to each individual what he has earned . . . and fixes the conditions on which this protection will be granted.'[37] The weakness of the pie theory is that there is no fixed sum to go round, that individuals add to the pie by their activities (the success of which may be very imperfectly correlated with effort, let alone merit) and that it is by no means obvious that others should treat the results as part of a common pool. Both theories have elements of validity, but there is no obvious compromise between them which is likely to be either logically or emotionally satisfying.

The equality suggested by the pie theory is, of course, notoriously difficult to define. Is it to be equality in relation to individuals or families, or needs? Is someone with greater capacity for happiness to be given more, as in some versions of utilitarianism, or less, to compensate for his inborn advantage? The complications are endless; and they are multiplied enormously once we abandon absolutes and talk about 'more equality' or 'less inequality'. The essential point has however been well stated by de Jouvenel : 'Every allocation of reward' which is founded 'on equality under a certain aspect, will be hierarchical and contrary to equality under another aspect'.[38]

Most popular discussions of relativities, 'national job evaluation' and similar notions are based on neither the pie nor the entitlement theory but on the very slippery idea of reward according to moral merit. The argument against this has been well stated by F. A. Hayek, who points out that, even if all inherited wealth or differences in educational opportunity could be abolished, there would still be no inherent moral value attaching to the resulting distribution of income and wealth :

> The inborn as well as the acquired gifts of a person clearly have a value to his fellows which does not depend on any credit due to him for possessing them. There is little a man can do to alter the fact that his special talents are very common or exceedingly rare. A good mind or a fine voice, a beautiful face or a skilful hand, a ready wit or an attractive personality are in a large measure as independent of a person's efforts as the opportunities or experiences he has had. In all these instances the value which a person's capacities or services have for us and for which he is recompensed has little relation to anything that we can call moral merit or deserts.[39]

Hayek argues that no man possesses the ability to determine conclusively the merits of another. To assess merit presupposes that a man has acted in accordance with some accepted rule of conduct and that someone else can judge how much effort and pain this has cost him. Often, of course, a highly meritorious attempt may be a complete failure, while a valuable human achievement will be due to luck or favourable circumstances. To decide on merit 'presupposes that we can judge whether people have made such use of their opportunities as they ought to have made, and how much effort of will or self-denial it had cost them and how much of their achievement is due to circumstances'. This is impossible in a free society or probably at all. (Moreover, only a fanatical ascetic would wish to encourage a maximum of merit in this sense. It is more rational for people 'to achieve a maximum of usefulness at a minimum of pain and sacrifice and therefore a minimum of merit.')

Indeed it is one of the advantages of a market economy enjoying basic bourgeois liberties that a man's livelihood does not depend on other people's valuation of his merit. It is sufficient that he should be able to perform some work or sell a service for which there is a demand. Hayek concedes that as an organisation grows larger it will become inevitable that ascertainable merit in the eyes of managers (or some conventional seniority structure) should determine rewards. But so long as there is no one single organisation with a comprehensive scale of merit, but a multiplicity of competing organisations with different practices (as well as smaller organisations and a self-employed sector), an individual still has a wider degree of freedom of choice.

Hayek is, however, wrong to suppose that all policies for redistribution of income and wealth inevitably involve assessing merit, measuring need or aiming to achieve equality of reward – whatever the latter would mean. There is another position. This is to accept the rankings of the actual or a reformed market but to use fiscal means to narrow differentials so that the game is played for smaller stakes. What is then needed is a view on the *general shape* of a tolerable distribution which does not involve a moralistic evaluation of any person or occupation.

One of the interests of Professor John Rawls's theory of justice is that, although he agrees with Hayek that reward based on supposed merit is neither desirable nor feasible, he nevertheless believes that the concept of social justice can be given a definite meaning. Rawls attempts to introduce an element of impartiality into the assessment of distribution by means of the 'veil of ignorance'. The idea is to work out the principles on which 'free and rational persons concerned to further their own interests' would desire their community to be run if they did not know their own social or economic place, the market value of their own talents and many other key features of their real situation.[40] A wealthy man might like to establish principles which minimise taxes for welfare purposes; a poor man might espouse principles of an opposite kind. If one excludes knowledge of one's own actual situation, there is some chance of working out the principles on a disinterested basis.

The Rawls theory is the most ambitious and serious modern attempt to construct a theory of social justice which neither attempts to assess merit nor to aim at complete equality but nevertheless seeks to provide criteria for state action in the field of income distribution and elsewhere. The 'maximum' principle, in which inequalities are justified if and only if they are to the advantage of the least well off, is at bottom a sophisticated version of the pie theory designed to take into account the effects of slicing on the size of the pie.

Yet, at least according to my reading of the critical literature, it has not succeeded. The basic flaw in the argument is the belief that a thought process under the 'veil of ignorance' must yield a unique result, and the consequent attempt to erect a dubious system of orderings and priorities which has kept the academic industry fully employed, if not 'overheated'. The 'veil of ignorance' is a very useful device for narrowing the range of disagreement, despite the imaginative leap required; but it cannot eliminate differences in subjective preferences. The varying hypothetical distributions which different people would support under the 'veil of ignorance' would reveal differences in attitudes to uncertainty. Someone with a taste for gambling would be interested in seeing that there were some really big incomes, just in case he came out lucky. One might hazard the guess that, if they were ignorant of their own position in the income distribution, most people would be concerned to 'level up' at the bottom so that there was no longer a depressed minority to which they might be consigned. Attitudes would, however, still differ a great deal towards the number and height of the summits at the upper end of the income distribution. Rawls himself agrees that, even if his principles are accepted, there is much room for disagreement about the range of social and economic inequalities which they actually justify.

Apart from the purely logical difficulties, it is doubtful if the Rawls scheme would ever have much popular appeal. A criticism which would probably be echoed by non-philosophers and non-economists, if they were following the discussion at all, is that, starting off as it does from calculations of rational self-interest, the Rawls theory contains very little 'justice' in the sense in which that word is normally used. Irving Kristol has pointed to the huge gap between Hayek's concept of a 'free society', in which we do not claim that position and reward depend on merit or work, and the traditional defences of capitalism, which asserted that they did.[41] But the contrast is equally great with a social democracy of the Rawls type based purely on what 'free and rational persons' might contract to do in their own self-interest.

Thus, if it is true that people do have, as Kristol argues, an emotional yearning for some quasi-theological justification for differences in position, power or well-being; if the rational arguments for accepting a system that does not aim at complete distributive justice are too abstract or sophisticated to command assent; and if there is an emotional void that cannot be met merely by rising incomes and humanitarian redistribution unrelated to 'merit', then the outlook for liberal democracy is a poor one.

One obvious gap in the preceding pages has been any specific scenario by which liberal democracy might disappear; and I have deliberately avoided discussing questions such as : 'Could the army become a political agency?' or 'What form might a middle-class revolt take?' The view that the present situation is unsustainable does not itself imply anything about the process of change or the nature of any new system.

There is no need to suppose that there will be an overnight coup; there could be a gradual process of disintegration of traditional political authority and the growth of new sources of power. Indeed, a continuation of present trends might lead to a situation where nothing remained of liberal democracy but its label. Nor need we assume that a new system will be repressive but efficient. It is just as easy to imagine a combination of pockets of anarchy combined with petty despotism, in which many of the amenities of life and the rule of law are absent, but in which there are many things which we will be prevented from doing or saying. Nor can we say whether the union problem will be tackled by right-wing authoritarian measures or by the unions themselves becoming the agents of repression in a People's Democracy. Let us not forget too that authoritarian regimes have their own weaknesses – above all those arising from the lack of effective criticism; and nothing that has been said in this paper implies that they will provide a stable solution. Above all, diagnosis is not historical prophecy. My conjecture about democracy could be forestalled by events or by preventive action. This is, after all, the point of making it. To point to weaknesses, tensions and dangers does not mean that we must succumb to them.

It would be presumptuous to add a 'blueprint for salvation' as a tailpiece or afterthought. In any case, the key to a more hopeful future lies in understanding rather than in blueprints. The most popular nostrum in the U.K. at the time of writing is a coalition or 'Government of National Unity'. Its advantage would be that it might do something about the generation of excessive expectations. If the leaders of the main parties shared responsibility, it would be difficult to pretend that all national difficulties sprang from the 'other side' being in power and that all would be well if there were a change of government. Those outside the coalition would be more likely to represent fundamentally different policies; and there would be no need for mainstream politicians to denigrate everything that goes on in the country for the half of the time that they are not in power.

The big disadvantage of a coalition is that it would tend to represent the conventional wisdom and wishful thinking of the hour, which would be even more difficult to displace than it is at present. Moreover, the process of outbidding could be eventually started up again by outside 'extremists', and disillusionment against all conventional politicians could eventually increase further. But there are occasions when it is worth buying time and I would stick to the judgement I made in 1968 that 'an experimental interval of coalition would be desirable'.[42] Some of the same considerations apply to a minority government depending on a (perhaps shifting) House of Commons coalition. The advantages of such an experiment do, however, depend on it being fairly broadly based and would apply in much smaller degree to a pure Con-Lib or Lab-Lib arrangement.

Nor, while on the subject of buying time, should one overlook the possibility of a change of economic luck. A favourable combination of events such as improved terms of trade, followed by good fortune from North Sea oil, would provide a better climate for the 'sharing out' functions of government than the last few years, in which expectations of growth have suffered a nasty jolt and economic policy has looked like a zero-sum game between different sections.

Yet it would be folly to depend on such once-for-all palliatives to do more than postpone the tendency of liberal democracy to generate unfulfillable expectations or the tensions arising from the pursuit of group self-interest. As the tensions spring from attitudes, it is in the realm of attitudes that a more enduring solvent will have to be found. Even an authoritarian government would be ultimately dependent on opinion, although perhaps the opinion of fewer or different people. As David Hume remarked,[43] 'The governors have nothing to support them but opinion. The Sultan of Egypt or the Emperor of Rome might drive his harmless subjects like brute beasts, against their sentiments and inclination; but he must at least have led his mamelukes or praetorian bands like men by their opinion.' It is, of course, not an easy matter to say in complex societies whose opinion counts and to what extent.

There is one tempting blind alley to avoid. Some philosophic conservatives trace the source of the contemporary malaise to the abandonment of the belief in absolute values and look back with nostalgia to the time when no one supposed that ordinary people were the best judges of their own happiness but it was taken for granted that such knowledge was available to a metaphysical, religious or political elite. Now, even if this is true as a diagnosis, it offers little hope of cure. For myths cannot hope to serve a social purpose if people know that they are myths and seek to preserve them in a utilitarian spirit. If God does not exist, He cannot be invented.

Many of our present tensions would become much less important in the unlikely event of a genuine revulsion against materialism or the 'consumer society'. Modern technology does make it possible to reduce the obsession with procuring ever more material products without having to submit to a life of ascetic poverty. It is unfortunate that the leadership among those who talk of an 'Alternative Society' should have been taken over by intolerant and envious political revolutionaries and that those most concerned with freedom, personal relations and the devising of new life styles for *themselves* should have lost ground. Perhaps the 'nice guys' who merely want to 'opt out' are bound to lose; but it would help if the forces of authority distinguished between the Angry Brigade and the left-wing student fascists on the one hand, and those primarily concerned to 'do their own thing' on the other.

Differences in status, because they lie in the eye of the beholder, are potentially both more disruptive and more emollient than material differences. If there is general agreement on what the top status positions are, combined with an intense desire to be at the top and a resentment of the way that it is recruited, then a great deal of tension can be predicted. By contrast, a society in which manual workers, professional and white-collar workers all regarded themselves as the true aristocrats would be good for people's self-respect. While not everyone can occupy the top income brackets, it would be possible for most people to value highly the activities that they themselves do; and the greater the range of human qualities that is admired, the less there need be feelings of inferiority. There is no exact or necessary correspondence between income or position in the productive process and other self-esteem or esteem in the eyes of others. But this is an area where opinion is all-important, and Marxists who insist on a one-dimensional model of satisfaction both help to make it true and increase the sum of human misery.

The ultimate sin of the politicians, the academics and the media has been their obsession with interpersonal and intergroup comparisons. This is seen in concepts such as 'relative deprivation' in sociology, 'inequality' (a loaded way of describing differences) and 'interdependent utilities' in economics, and 'equal freedom' in political philosophy. It is no use saying that resentment and envy of the possessions and achievements of others, and strong views about people's life-styles, simply exist whether the liberal individualists likes it or not. The attitudes in question are influenced by what is said and written; and the contribution of the so-called intelligentsia is to focus all attention on relativities to the exclusion of absolutes. Moreover, their object in so doing is not to stir up personal rivalry and emulation, which add to the interests and joys, as well as the unhappiness, of life; it is to emphasise differences while asserting that they should

131

not be there. The result is to reinforce the type of envious self-defeating attitudes revealed by the U.K. Survey Research Unit, in which 80 per cent of those questioned said they would rather receive an extra £4 a week in common with everyone else than receive an extra £5, if everyone else's income were to rise by the still higher sum of £6.[44]

If comparisons are always with other people, and never with past achievements, the hope of progress is at an end; and what the pessimistic theologians have failed to do will have been achieved by the secular egalitarians. If we look at definite things, such as treatment of children, the level of nutrition, health, housing or consumption of the poorest, or the efficiency and humanity of the penal system, improvement is possible. In the realm of intangibles such as self-respect and regard for others, improvement is more difficult but can still be envisaged; and this also applies to the reduction of coercion in human affairs. But if all that matters is whether other people are better or worse off than oneself in these respects, then human history is a zero-sum game. Even if the principle of diminishing marginal utility is misapplied to assert that the gains of those who moved up are greater than the losses of those who move down, then all advance stops when equality has been reached; and, as has already been pointed out, the definition of that state is far from obvious and likely to cause extreme acrimony, with most people feeling that they have been treated less equally than others.

Quite apart from these conceptual difficulties, there is no reason to suppose that any target reduction in 'inequality' (or even in the share of property income) would supply a basis of consent to the social or economic structure. Indeed, the more that policy concentrates on eliminating disparities and differentials, the greater the sense of outrage likely to be engendered by those that remain. Moreover, the smaller the financial contrast between the mass of wage and salary earners and the wealthy minority, the greater the attention that is likely to be paid to relativities among workers. As it is,

90 per cent of consumer spending comes from wages, salaries and social security payments, and the annual wage round is to a large extent a contest between different groups of workers for relative shares. It is one of the defects of the present preoccupation with differentials, whether from a desire to establish an 'incomes policy' or from a wish to iron out 'inequality', that each group becomes much more keenly aware of what other groups are obtaining and more critical of the basis of comparison, which can always be made in more than one way; and this increases rather than diminishes the ferocity of the struggle.

The ideal of equality has had a noble role in human history. It has served to assert that all men and women are entitled to respect, and to rally people against oppression. But it has now turned sour. Liberal democracy will not be saved by detailed policy programmes which will soon be overtaken by events. It could yet be saved if contemporary egalitarianism were to lose its hold over the intelligentsia. But this will happen only if those who recognise it for the disease it has become are prepared to come out in the open and have uncongenial labels placed upon them, as well as to consort with strange bedfellows on whom a watchful eye will always have to be kept.

## NOTES

1  This chapter was originally presented as a paper to Section F of the British Association at its 1974 Annual Meeting. It subsequently appeared in a substantially revised form in the *British Journal of Political Science,* 5 (1975), 129–59. The present chapter is a shortened version of the *British Journal* article.

2  It is, of course, possible to define self-interest in such a way that it covers all the goals people can possibly seek, whether individually or collectively. Such an approach lies behind the modern formal 'economic' theories of democracy. For a recent attempt at a synthesis of such theories see Albert Breton, *The Economic Theory of Representative Government* (London: Macmillan, 1974).

3  I am indebted to Bertrand de Jouvenel for suggesting this term (in a private communication).

4  My own view of what Western societies could and should attempt to achieve can be found in S. Brittan, *Capitalism and the Permissive Society* (London: Macmillan, 1973).

5  Joseph A. Schumpeter, *Capitalism, Socialism and Democracy,* 4th edn. (London: Allen and Unwin, 1952), Part IV, p. 269.

6  Plamenatz is probably right to argue that the 'popular' theory of democracy is a better name than Schumpeter's own term 'classical'. See John Plamenatz, *Democracy and Illusion: an Examination of Certain Aspects of Modern Democratic Theory* (London: Longman, 1973), p. 39.

7  For a discussion of this issue, see David Butler and Donald Stokes, *Political Change in Britain: Forces Shaping Electoral Choice* (Harmondsworth, Middx.: Penguin Books, 1971), Chaps. 8 and 9 (pp. 217–64). Also, for a confirmation of the low level of political awareness in the USA from the 'Michigan School', see Angus Campbell, Philip E. Converse, Warren E. Miller and Donald E. Stokes, *The American Voter* (New York: Wiley, 1960), pp. 60–1, 151.

8  Butler and Stokes, *Political Change*, Chaps. 8 and 9.

9 For a notable recent example, which contains references to nearly all the principal works of this school, see fn 2.

10 Above all that of Gustave Le Bon, *The Crowd* (London: T. Fisher Unwin, 1896, rep. 1917).

11 Schumpeter, *Capitalism, Socialism*, p. 263.

12 Schumpeter, *Capitalism, Socialism*, p. 262.

13 'Psychological and Administrative Barriers to Voting', *Report of the President's Commission on Registration and Voting Participation* (Washington, D.C.: U.S. Government Printing Office, 1963). Reprinted in *Political Opinion and Electoral Behaviour: Essays and Studies*, eds. Edward Dreyer and Walter A. Rosenbaum (Belmont, Calif.: Wadsworth, 1966), pp. 174–80.

14 NOP, *Britain Today*, p. 6.

15 NOP, *Political Bulletin*, September 1974.

16 For a preliminary report, see Mark Abrams, 'This Britain: A Contented Nation?', *New Society*, 21 February 1974.

17 These influences are discussed in W. G. Runciman, *Relative Deprivation and Social Justice: a Study of Attitudes to Social Inequalities in Twentieth Century England* (London: Routledge, 1966), Chaps. 2 and 4.

18 NOP, *Political Bulletin*, March/April 1974. There was little variation through the social and income groups. The proportion rose to 42 per cent for those earning above £4,000 per annum in the pounds of that period – a category not large enough to provide significant sums.

19 See Brittan and *Second Thoughts on Full Employment*. (Chichester: Barry Rose).

20 His principal article on the subject is entitled 'How inflation threatens: British democracy's last chance before extinction' (*The Times*, 1 July 1974). Other relevant articles by Jay are 'Incomes policy: cycles of failure' (27 June 1973) and 'The good old days of stop-go economies' (5 December 1973). *Times* 'leaders' supplying useful background include 'Social Democrats and Inflation' (5 December 1973) and 'The Great Priority' (23 July 1974).

21   See Brittan, *Steering the Economy*, pp. 207–19 and 479–83.

22   A. V. Dicey, *Law and Public Opinion in England* (London: Macmillan, 1963), pp. 152–8.

23   Quoted in E. Halévy, *A History of the English People in the Nineteenth Century, Vol VI: The Rule of Democracy 1905–1914*, Book II (London: Ernest Benn, 1952), p. 486.

24   *Report of the Transport Workers' Court of Inquiry* (London: HMSO, Cmd. 936, 1970), Vol I, p. 495.

25   W. Bagehot, *The English Constitution* (London: Fontana edition, with introduction by R. H. S. Crossman, 1963), pp. 267–310.

26   J. A. Froude, *Address to the Liberty and Property Defence League* (London: Liberty and Property Defence League, 1887).

27   Schumpeter, *Capitalism, Socialism*, p. 291.

28   Schumpeter, *Capitalism, Socialism*, p. 294.

29   Schumpeter, *Capitalism, Socialism*, p. 293.

30   Irving Kristol, 'When Virtue Loses her Loveliness', Chap. 1 of *Capitalism Today*, ed. Irving Kristol and Daniel Bell (New York: Mentor Books, 1971), pp. 13–27.

31   Kristol, *Capitalism Today*, p. 19.

32   F. A. Hayek, *The Constitution of Liberty* (London: Routledge, 1960), Chap. 6, pp. 85–100.

33   Bertrand de Jouvenel, *Sovereignty* (Chicago: University of Chicago Press, 1957), p. 284.

34   De Jouvenel, *Sovereignty*, Chap. 16, pp. 184–7.

35   John Goldthorpe, 'Social Inequality and Social Integration in Modern Britain', in *Poverty, Inequality and Class Structure*, ed. D. Wedderburn (Cambridge: Cambridge University Press, 1974), Chap. 11, pp. 117–38.

36   Robert Nozick, 'Distributive Justice', *Philosophy and Public Affairs*, III (1973), 45–126, p. 45.

37   Froude, *Address*.

38   De Jouvenel, *Sovereignty*, p. 151.

39   Hayek, *The Constitution of Liberty*, Chap. 6.

40   John Rawls, *A Theory of Justice* (Oxford: Clarendon Press, 1972), p. 11.

41   Kristol, in *Capitalism Today*, pp. 16–22.

42   Samuel Brittan, *Left or Right: The Bogus Dilemma* (London: Secker and Warburg, 1968), p. 166.

43   David Hume, *Essay on the First Principles of Government* (Oxford: Oxford University Press, 1963), p. 29.

44   Abrams, 'This Britain'.

# Afterword

If the reader of this book has been keeping track, he will have noticed that the five contributors to it have offered somewhere between ten and twenty different explanations and part-explanations of why Britain is becoming harder to govern. They range from Coates's belief that we are in the midst of a crisis of capitalism to St John-Stevas's belief in the importance of the decline in religious belief, from my own and Brittan's emphasis on the crucial role of the level of mass expectations to Mackintosh's belief that much can be explained by the disintegration of the old parliamentary 'consent model'.

It would be pleasing at this stage to be able to combine all five contributors' explanations to form some single, over-arching answer to our central question. But of course it would be quite wrong to do so. Not only do the various contributors disagree among themselves (St John-Stevas would be unlikely to accept Coates's theory of capitalist crisis); they have not addressed themselves to the problem of what the causal relationships may be among the various explanations they offer. What, for example, is the connection between the unrestrained 'pursuit of group self-interest in the market place', to which Brittan refers, and the new concepts of legitimacy, which Mackintosh discusses? Is either caused by the other? Or are both the result of a general 'crisis of authority'?

Lest, however, the reader be overwhelmed by the number and diversity of the explanations that have been offered, he should take note of several rather obvious explanations that have not been offered. The five essays in this book are at least as striking for what they leave out as for what they contain.

In the first place, none of our five contributors sets out to place the blame for our troubles on the Conservative party, or on the Labour party, or even on the two main political parties taken together. John Mackintosh, the Labour MP, and Norman St John-Stevas, the Conservative MP, both accept that Governments of both parties have been at fault in the recent past and, more to the point, that both parties are to a large extent subject to attitudes and forces they cannot control. To be sure, Brittan suggests that the temporary suspension of party politics and the formation of a broadly based coalition Government might help to buy Britain time, and that the time thus bought might be worth having, but he quickly goes on to repeat his central point that the pursuit of group self-interest, which is at the root of our troubles, is a consequence of people's attitudes and is not to be blamed on party politics as such. It is implicit in both Brittan's chapter and my own that a party realignment by itself would not be of much use, since any set of competitive political parties, however it was aligned, would have to respond to the same attitudes and pressures that the Conservative and Labour parties do now.

If the political parties are not to blame, neither, according to our contributors, are 'subversives' or 'red revolutionaries'. They exist, of course; Coates, though he might reject these particular labels, would probably be happy to be counted amongst them. But it is striking how seldom they have appeared in these pages. They are scarcely referred to in four of the five chapters and in the fifth, Mackintosh's, are dismissed in three short paragraphs. In Mackintosh's view, the truly anti-system elements in the community are weak both in numbers and in influence. They should be understood, not as an explanation of why Britain is becoming harder to govern, but simply as one manifestation, not a very important one, of the widespread lack of respect for traditional authority in our society. Some readers may feel that the power of the 'irreconcilables and revolutionaries', as Mackintosh calls them, has been underestimated in this book. One can only record that any of our contributors could have offered them as a major part of his explanation, and that none did.

But perhaps the most remarkable single omission from our contributors' catalogue of explanations is the trade unions. Or, rather, the trade unions are included, but only under the heading of groups that pursue their own interests and may fail to act in conformity with the wishes of Governments – a very general heading that takes in not only trade unions but also (to judge from the pages of this book) multinational companies, the Organisation of Petroleum Exporting Countries, dairy farmers, ratepayers and even mass electorates. The trade unions may be more powerful than some of these groups, but they are less powerful than others (notably OPEC) and in any case are not unique. If this general view is accepted, what needs explaining is not why the trade unions in Britain sometimes appear to be more assertive than those in other countries but rather why group rivalries in general in Britain are so intense.

Indeed, if there is one thread that ties together all of the chapters in this book, it is that the blame for our troubles should not be placed on individuals or groups of individuals. The search for scapegoats is bound to be fruitless and should be abandoned. Our troubles cannot simply be laid at the door of militant trade unionists, or multinational corpora-, tions, or subversive elements, or socialists, or the Tory party. Rather, all of our contributors agree, Britain is becoming harder to govern because of faults lying somewhere in 'the system' – in the relationships of individuals to the means of production and to one another. Scapegoats, if they were found, could be eliminated; but, on this analysis, the country's problems would remain. Where our contributors differ, of course, is in the features of the system to which they draw attention and which they believe to be crucial. Coates believes that the relevant system is the capitalist, Brittan that the relevant system is the system of competitive pluralism which has developed in Britain in recent years and which might continue to exist (and indeed might even get worse) if Britain's economy ceased to be capitalist.

It will not have escaped the reader's attention that this has been a very Britain-centred book. In one sense, this was inevitable. The question we asked our authors was : Why is *Britain* becoming harder to govern? But in another sense it is unfortunate. For one thing, unless we compare Britain with other countries, we have no way of knowing for sure whether our conclusions about Britain are correct. It may be that some of the factors cited in this book to account for the difficulties of this country also manifest themselves in other countries without producing the same results. For example, to quote Brittan again, there would seem on the face of it to be nothing peculiarly British about 'the pursuit of group self-interest in the market place'. Why, then, does this pursuit seem to have so much more serious effects in Britain than elsewhere? Similarly, it is not altogether clear from Coates's analysis why 'the crisis of capitalism' should have come so early to Britain, or how soon it can be expected to overtake other countries.

This concentration on Britain has another unfortunate consequence. Not only does it render uncertain the force of explanations of what is happening to Britain, it also has the effect of failing to alert one to the possibility, indeed the probability, that other countries are becoming harder to govern too. Certainly, many of the developments described in this book – the decline in support for established political parties, the growth of 'direct action' tactics on the part of pressure groups, the disappearance of a religious and moral consensus – can be observed equally well abroad. It would be interesting to know just how peculiar Britain is. Maybe Britain, with its powerfully organised interest groups and national media of communication, constitutes the wave of the future and that the difficulties experienced by British Governments in recent years will be experienced more and more frequently by Governments overseas. The 'English sickness' may not be contagious; but its virus may well be present in other bodies politick.

If it is accepted that Britain is becoming harder to govern, and if it is agreed that the people of Britain would be better off if it were easier to govern, what is to be done? Our contributors did not have this question put to them directly, but most of them offered brief answers to it all the same. Their answers run the gamut from overthrowing the capitalist system (Coates) through an ending of our obsession with interpersonal comparisons (Brittan) to various forms of tinkering with the machinery of government (King, St John-Stevas and Mackintosh). One possible answer, however, was given by none of the contributors. None of them maintained that we should envisage putting an end to our system of parliamentary democracy. In the words of Brittan, 'the point of saying that a house is on fire is to alert the fire brigade, not to sit back and enjoy the blaze.' Quite apart from liberal democracy's intrinsic value, there is no reason whatever to believe that, if Britain ceased to be a democracy, she would become either easier to govern or more successful economically. The world is littered with the wreckage of inefficient dictatorships.

# Contributors

## Anthony King

He has been Professor of Government at the University of Essex since 1969. Born in Canada, he was a Rhodes Scholar at Oxford and then a Fellow of Magdalen College. With David Butler he wrote two studies of the general elections of 1964 and 1966. He is currently editor of the *British Journal of Political Science*.

## David Coates

After taking his D.Phil. at Oxford, David Coates went to teach politics at York University. He is currently researching trends in postwar industrial relations in Britain and the character of leadership in working-class political and industrial organisations. He has published *The Labour Party and the Struggle for Socialism* (1975) and *Teachers' Unions and Interest Group Politics* (1972).

## Norman St John-Stevas

He has been Conservative MP for Chelmsford since 1964, and is at present Conservative spokesman on education and the arts. He is a barrister, former Fellow of Yale Law School and a journalist who has written extensively for *The Economist*. He is the author of a biography of Walter Bagehot as well as the editor of his collected works.

*John P. Mackintosh*

Educated at Edinburgh, Oxford and Princeton universities, he became Professor of Politics at the University of Strathclyde in 1965. He is the author of *The British Cabinet* (1962), *The Devolution of Power* (1968) and *British Government and Politics* (1970). He has been Labour MP for Berwick and East Lothian since 1966, except for a few months in 1974.


*Samuel Brittan*

A writer for the *Financial Times*. He was the first winner of the senior Wincott Award for financial journalists and is a Visiting Fellow of Nuffield College, Oxford. He is the author of *Steering the Economy* (1971), *Capitalism and the Permissive Society* (1973) and *Second Thoughts on Full Employment Policy* (1975)